Group
Playing
Words

Group Games
Playing with Words

ROSEMARIE PORTMAN &
ELISABETH SCHNEIDER

Speechmark

Speechmark Publishing Ltd
Telford Road • Bicester • Oxon OX26 4LQ • United Kingdom

Originally published in German by Don Bosco Verlag München under the title *Mit Sprache spielen* © Don Bosco Verlag, München 1997

Published in 2005 by
Speechmark Publishing Ltd, Telford Road, Bicester, Oxon OX26 4LQ, UK
Telephone +44 (0)1869 244644   Facsimile +44 (0)1869 320040
www.speechmark.net

© Speechmark Publishing Ltd, 2005

002-5271/Printed in the United Kingdom/1010

British Library Cataloguing in Publication Data

Portmann, Rosemarie
   Playing with words. – (Group Games) (A Speechmark practical activity resource)
   1. Group play therapy 2. Word games
   I. Title II. Schneider, Elisabeth
   615.8'5153

ISBN-10: 0 86388 545 4
ISBN-13: 978 0 86388 545 7

Contents

About the Authors

Rosemarie Portmann Dip (Psychol) is the manager of the educational psychology service for the local education authority in Wiesbaden, Germany. She is also an adviser to the Parents Association in Hessen.

Rosemarie is a lecturer at the Institute for Educational Pedagogy and Teaching Methods in the Elementary and Primary Department of the University of Frankfurt.

She is the author of several successful games books and other specialist publications, including *Emotional Strength & Self-Esteem* and *Dealing with Aggression,* and co-author with Elisabeth Schneider of *Relaxation & Concentration*, all in the 'Group Games' series, which are also published by Speechmark.

Elisabeth Schneider is the pedagogical head of a comprehensive school in Giessen.

Acknowledgements

Thank you to Lilo Seelos, the translator.

Note: The text sometimes refers to the leader or the child as 'he', for the sake of clarity alone.

Games

Introduction

Playing makes children brighter and happier. Moreover, the simplest and invariably the cheapest toy available is our language. All you need in order to supplement language is a pencil and paper, perhaps a few old newspapers, and you are ready to start.

Occupying oneself with letters, words and text can be creative and enjoyable and does not just mean tedious hours learning spelling, or the reading and writing of boring texts. Anyone who engages with language in a playful way will, over time, have fewer literacy problems, become interested in reading, and discover literary skills they did not know they possessed.

ABOUT THE SELECTION OF GAMES

This collection is a colourful mix of games and suggested variations, ranging from creative writing to tried and trusted word and language exercises. The collection is so extensive that there will be something new and suitable for every group and every occasion.

Players can contribute to the activities, such as making letter or word cards, preparing riddles or joke questions, or cutting something out of a newspaper.

The games can be used at any time and in any place, perhaps making use of ten minutes of relaxation time during a lesson or a seminar, or providing creative work for group activities, camps, adult education and relaxation, whether these take place in a room, on a bus or a train, or even outside in a field. Some of the games require minimal time, others can be played for as long as you want. There are no limits set on the imagination of the players. The rules can be made easier, more difficult, or changed completely, depending on the needs and skills of the players, but they should always be clearly spelled out and agreed by the group at the beginning of a game.

The majority of the games are suitable for anyone and any size of group, ensuring that no member of the group ever has to sit out. However, many of the games are equally enjoyable when played by a single person or a pair.

The games have been devised so that they do not have to be played competitively – no one needs to win or lose – but suggestions are given for adapting the games to 'play to win' situations, even if the players (as yet) only have limited reading and writing skills.

The games are primarily intended to be playtime fun where everyone participates. But playing with language also sharpens the intellect. Many of the games can also be used educationally and therapeutically to achieve specific learning goals. Comments are inserted into the games to outline their use for improving communication. The most important factor for including a game in this collection, however, is the fun that the games provide. A game has to be fun – otherwise it is not a good game!

HOW TO USE THE GAMES

The games should not turn into compulsory exercises, run by majority decisions. Even in a group, only those people who really feel like playing should 'have' to play. This is particularly true when playing the games at school. If someone does not want to play, they should be allowed to watch quietly, without disturbing the game. Most onlookers will eventually be drawn into the game of their own volition. If possible, the group should try to agree on a game which everybody who wants to can play.

The first round of each game generally tends to be a trial run. If it does not work, the description of the game should be read again carefully. Game variations, rules and valuations can now be altered. However, the rules have to be clearly and exactly defined before every round. Playing is only fun if everything works out in the end.

The question of whether there needs to be a game leader and whether the leader can play too, depends on several factors, including the make-up of the group and the type of game chosen. Some groups, especially those consisting of younger children, require a neutral person, who helps, comforts and mediates. Some games require someone to give instructions and control the course of the game. If the leaders are not playing, they should try to stay in the background and only intervene if the game situation demands it.

When selecting a particular game, the time required to play the game needs to be considered. Games should not be too long to ensure that the players do not tire of them. On the other hand, games should not be stopped at any time because the time to play has run out. Playing will only be beneficial and encourage groups to play more games, if the group members feel quite content and relaxed at the end of each game.

The Games

a-e-i-o-u

This game has as many rounds as there are vowels, ie, five. In the first round every player writes down as many nouns as possible containing only the vowel 'a'. In the second round, players write down as many nouns as they can think of containing only the vowel 'e', and so on.

Round 1:   cat, can, band, bag, sack, tack …
Round 2:   wren, rest, hen, bell, beg, leg, degree …
Round 3:   tin, wink, sink, bin, bliss, knitting …
Round 4:   boss, dog, rot, Bob, mob, top …
Round 5:   mud, bus, turn, sun, bun, nun, nut …

Game variations:

◆ Many more words can be found if every type of word is used. Longer and more unusual words can be created by allowing compound words:

a: aardvark ad
e: Lee's teeth
i: Mississippi fish
o: dog dollop
u: sunburnt mum

◆ The number of rounds can be extended if players have to find words which only contain a certain vowel combination:

ea: bean; dead …
ee: beer; deed …
ia: liar; Brian …
io: lion; onion …
ai: paid; lair …
ay: day; bray …
ou: bought; sought …
oa: loan; moan …
oi: coin; loin …
oo: book; food …
oy: toy; boy …

◆ Instead of words, the players could also write down short sentences containing only a particular vowel. The number of words in a sentence could be set at a given number. The example below shows a minimum of three words:

a: Barbara bans bats.
e: Ben sweeps seeds.
i: Big Bird sings.
o: Otto lost food.
u: Nuns gulp gum.

◆ Another alternative is to find words that contain as few as possible additional vowels to the targeted vowel:

a: baggage
e: benevolent
i: billion
o: footnote
u: rupture

The winner is the person who gets the most words containing the target vowel per round. Bonus points could be given for the longest word, or the longest sentence with the same vowel. If additional vowels were allowed, their number is deducted from the number of target vowels used.

(2) Everything OK?

Abbreviations demand to be played with! It can be lots of fun to give new meaning to common abbreviations. For example:

OK: old kebab, or orange King …
TV: the vestry, or thin vegans …
VIP: virtually impenetrable palace, or Vick's invisible poodle …

Game variations

◆ One player thinks of the abbreviations and the others each have to find, within an agreed time, as many funny new interpretations as possible.

◆ Instead of abbreviations, the players could also use car number plates and make up imaginative phrases or short sentences.

> The winner is the person who has the most or the funniest ideas.

3 Everything you can eat beginning with R

A category and an initial letter are chosen. Players have to think of as many items belonging to the given category starting with the chosen letter. For example:

Everything you can eat beginning with:

R: radishes, rhubarb, ribs, raisins ...

S: swede, sausages, sweets, sugar ...

Game variation

◆ Now add a second letter after the first and make the game more difficult, such as everything you can eat beginning with:

Sp: Spaghetti, spam, spearmint, spinach, spices ...

Be: beetroot, beans, berries ...

If players are writing down their own items, five points could be given for each word that no one else has thought of, and perhaps only one point for words that have also been thought of by others. The person who has the most points after a certain number of rounds is the winner. Alternatively, the winner could be the player who thought of the most words in a given time, or who thought of a certain number of words fastest. Bonus points could be given for more original or creative word solutions.

(4) Alphabet stories number 1

Every player writes a story in which the first word starts with A, the second with B, the third with C, and so on, until Z. The players can agree to leave out difficult letters like Q, X and Y. For example:

All bad chameleons don't ever find good ...

Game variations

◆ The alphabet is used backwards, for example:

Zany, wicked vampires undertake tricky scary ...

◆ Players invent the story together with each player taking a turn to add a word. The story can be as long as you like. After the last word beginning with Z is reached start again with the letter A, or vice versa if starting from the end of the alphabet.

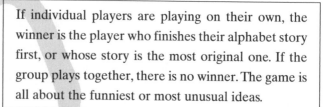

If individual players are playing on their own, the winner is the player who finishes their alphabet story first, or whose story is the most original one. If the group plays together, there is no winner. The game is all about the funniest or most unusual ideas.

5 Alphabet stories number 2

Players take turns to tell or write down a short sentence for a coherent story about a previously agreed topic. Each sentence starts with consecutive letters of the alphabet. The players could agree to leave out difficult letters such as Q, X and Y and perhaps even K. For example:

The topic is a visit to the cinema.

Anna went to the cinema.
Ben wanted to go with her.
'**C**hildren are not allowed to see this film', said Anna to Ben.
'**D**arling sister, why can't we see a different film?', asked Ben.

Game variations

♦ The first noun of each sentence rather than the first word of each sentence, has to start with consecutive letters of the alphabet. For example:

The topic is 'friends'

Anna is a young girl.
And **B**etty is her best friend.
Both love to eat **c**ake.
Every **d**ay they go swimming together.

Stories either have to be finished by the time the end of the alphabet is reached or the players could go through the alphabet twice. Perhaps once they have reached Z, they can go backwards, finishing at A. Alternatively, the story can continue until the players cannot think of any suitable new sentences.

This game is great fun if everybody just plays it together without scoring points. If individual players or small groups are playing against each other, the stories are written down, read aloud, and a prize is given for the most original story.

6 Alphabet stories number 3

One word for each letter of the alphabet is chosen at random from a newspaper or magazine. The word is written down on a piece of paper by all the players. X, Z and any other tricky letters can be left out. Once all the words have been found, each player uses them to write a story. Players are not allowed to add any new words, but they can alter verb tenses and make nouns singular or plural. For example:

A – Birmingham – chameleon – do – evening – fight – garden – hat – in – Jack – kicking – late – men – naughty – one – past – queen – ride – said – the – ugly – various – with – young – zebra

The (rather laboured) story could read:

One evening in a Birmingham garden, Jack kicked ugly chameleons. 'Don't! Naughty!', said the queen riding past. Later, young men with hats fought various zebras.

Game variations
◆ Allow the players to use as many 'helping' words as they like, such as pronouns, conjunctions, prepositions, articles and so on. The players are allowed to use the given words more than once, but are not allowed to add new words.

◆ Before play begins, players should agree whether the story is going to be a thriller, a love story, a report, and so on. With younger children, it is better if they play together, rather than against each other. In this case, the game leader might also be allowed to exchange a word which cannot be used.

When all the players have finished, the stories are read out. The best story (chosen by the participants) is given a prize.

7 Anagrams

Players have to find words whose letters can be rearranged to make a new, meaningful word. For example:

real – earl
golf – flog
reed – deer

The longer the words become, the more difficult the game gets. Only real experts will work out such splendid anagrams as: saddening herd – hidden gardens. It would be best to keep it simple!

Game variation

◆ Name anagrams of well-known figures are easier:

Who, for example, might Alan den Moslen be?
(Nelson Mandela)

And who is Rachel Chaumchiems?
(Michael Schumacher)

And Robert Sajilu?
(Julia Roberts)

Depending on the game variation played, the winner is either the player who has found the most anagrams within a given time, or who has managed to rearrange an anagram to its original word or name.

8 Anagrams with leftovers

New words are made from a random selection of words, with as few leftover letters as possible:

apple – plea + P
sight – hits + G
recipe – price + E

Game variations

◆ By adding to or swapping one letter of the original word the game can be made more difficult:

Adding	*Swapping*
coal – local (+ L)	lamb – malt (T instead of B)
ink – king (+ G)	open – pond (D instead of E)

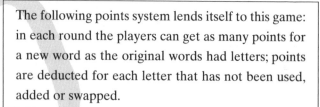

The following points system lends itself to this game: in each round the players can get as many points for a new word as the original words had letters; points are deducted for each letter that has not been used, added or swapped.

9 Analogies

A pair of words with a semantic connection is given. For a second pair of words which have a similar connection, only one word is shown. The players have to find a partner for this word.

horse – stable   car – ? (eg, garage)
hungry – eating   thirsty – ? (eg, drinking)
day – light   night – ? (eg, dark)

Game variations

◆ Players take turns: the first player thinks of a word, while the next responds with a similar word, then thinks of a new pair of words, and so on.

◆ The group leader provides a written list of the analogies to be worked out, and the players solve the task in writing.

Depending on the game variation, the attraction of this game lies in matching similar words. The winner could be the player who has managed to find the most analogies within a given time, or the player who was fastest to solve a set of analogies.

Beginning and ending

Players must find words from the initial and last letters chosen by the leader. For example, within a given time, all players have to write down as many words as possible that begin with B and end in N such as:

bea**n** – **b**i**n** – **b**u**n** – **b**urde**n** - **b**etwee**n** …

Game variation

◆ The game can be made less or more difficult depending on the chosen letter combination. For example, it is much more difficult to find words that start with B but end in K such as:

brick – **b**oo**k** – **b**lack …

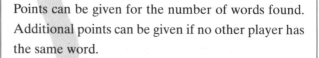

Points can be given for the number of words found. Additional points can be given if no other player has the same word.

11 Article hunt

Players think of words that contain the definite article 'the', such as:

theatre – hea**the**r – soo**the** ...

Game variations

◆ The game becomes a lot easier if players look for words containing the indefinite articles 'a' and 'an':

A: **a**pple – b**a**th – cinem**a** ...
An: **an**t – ban**an**a – b**an** ...

◆ Words could also be restricted to a particular word group (ie, nouns, verbs, fruit, names) to make the game more difficult.

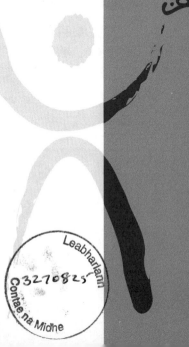

(12) Associations

Within a given time, players have to find as many associations for a particular word as possible: they should be associations that can be understood by all players. The word can either be chosen by the game leader, or the group can choose a word together. Possible examples of associations for 'chair' and 'bicycle' are:

Chair: leg – table – corridor – rocking – sitting – hard, and so on.

Bicycle: wheel – saddle – sport – cyclist – shorts – race.

Game variations

◆ Players don't play to a given time, but as soon as the first player has thought of ten associations, they call out 'stop', and everybody has to stop.

◆ Players agree in advance what type of words are allowed: for example, nouns only.

◆ The game becomes more difficult if the initial letter of each new word has to be the same as the final letter of the preceding word. For example: chair – rest – table, and so on.

Depending on the game variation, points can be given either for the number of words or for their originality.

13) 'Wig' rhymes with 'twig'

As many rhyming words as possible have to be found for a particular word. For example, if the chosen word is wig, rhyming words could be: big – twig – fig …

Game variations

◆ Two or more players take turns to find a new rhyming word. A player who cannot think of another rhyming word drops out of that round until one player is left.

◆ The length of the rhyming words is determined by the starting word. If the starting word has only four letters, the rhyming words must also contain only four letters. For example: dive – hive – jive – live, and so on …

◆ Players only look for word pairs that rhyme. The first player chooses a word, for which the next player has to think of a rhyme, before providing his neighbour with a new word for the next rhyming pair:

Player 1: dog
Player 2: frog. Suggests: dance
Player 3: lance. Suggests: mice
Player 4: lice. Suggests: pinch
and so on, around the group.

Depending on the game variation, points can be given for the number of rhyming words found within a given time, or for the originality of the words. Alternatively, the winner could be the player who was the last person to think of a rhyming word.

14 'Slip' becomes 'snap'

Players try to make word chains, starting with a word with four letters. Change one letter at a time to make a new word. Starting with the word 'slip', for example, the word chain is created by changing one letter at a time, and could look like this:

slip
flip
flop
slop
sop
sap
slap
snap

Game variations

- ◆ Every player makes his own word chain, Players are either given a word limit or a time limit.

- ◆ Players are divided into groups. Players take it in turns to find a new word within each group.

If everybody plays together, the winner could be the player who is the last person to think of a letter change: the others are out one at a time as they fail to think of a word. Alternatively, the winners could be decided by the time needed to find a given number of words, a number of words within a given time, or the uniqueness and originality of the words.

15 Categories

One player closes their eyes and points to a word in a newspaper or book. The letters of that word are then written, one under another, on a piece of paper. A category of words is also decided. The players now have to think of as many words as possible which start with the letters of the chosen word and belong to a category (chosen by the group).

For example, the word is 'swim'. The category chosen is names of cities and towns.

S	Southampton
	Sydney
	Seattle
W	Washington
	Wagga Wagga
	Warsaw
I	Indianapolis
	Inverness
	Istanbul
M	Manchester
	Memphis
	Montreal

Game variation

◆ The word picked at random could also determine the category. For example, if the word happens to be a first name, as many (male or female) first names as possible have to be found for each letter of that name. For example:

C Callum – Christopher – Chapal …
A Anthony – Andrew – Archie …
R Rolf – Richard – Rex …
L Luke – Liam – Lalit …

◆ Two or more players could play as a team to compensate for knowledge and speed differences.

The winner is the person who finds the most words within a given time. More points are given for words which have only been named by one player.

16 Engaged

The group or the group leader decides on a subject area. Each player lists nine random terms relating to that subject on their own piece of paper. The group leader then calls out as many words as he can think of that relate to the given subject. If a player has written down one of the words called out by the leader, they cross it out from their list. When three words have been crossed out, the player calls out 'three' and for six words, 'six'. When all the words are crossed out, the player calls out 'engaged'. For example, if the subject area is European countries:

Player A writes: England, Belgium, France, Norway, Yugoslavia, Spain, Italy, Austria, Monaco ...

Player B writes: England, Holland, Portugal, Switzerland, Italy, Finland, Ireland, Hungary ...

The leader then begins to go through his/her list:

Finland (B can cross out a word, A can't)
Italy (A and B can cross out a word)
Switzerland (B can cross out a word, A can't)

B calls out 'three!', because he has already crossed out three words, and so on.

Game variations
◆ Each player writes down a maximum of six words.

◆ Together, the group comes up with a list of possible words relating to the subject area. From this list, each player secretly chooses a given number of words. The leader then calls out words from the list in a random order. Smaller groups could also play against each other.

> While the game assumes a certain knowledge of the subject area, winning is a matter of chance: it is always the first player to call out 'engaged'.

(**17**) Bridging words

The group leader provides two words for which the players have to find a bridging word, which can provide both the ending of the first word and the beginning of the second word. For example:

> short – **cut** – lass
> tea – **spoon** – fed

Game variations

◆ Players could also think of the words connected by the bridging word.

◆ Players decide to allow compound words, which are written as individual words, for example, 'ball gown'.

◆ The bridging words game can be made even more challenging. The group leader provides a list of words for which the initial letters of the bridging words themselves can be combined into a meaningful word. For example, the first letter of each bridging word has to make a word for something found in the kitchen:

> light – **h**ouse – maid
> roll – **o**ver – board
> tooth – **b**rush – stroke

The kitchen item is 'hob'.

(18) Letter Patience

Letters of a clearly readable size are cut out of newspapers or catalogues and stuck onto small cards which should all be identical in size. The cards are shuffled and distributed. Each player now tries to use their own letters to make meaningful words. The aim is to use up as many letters as possible. For example:

One player has the letters:
A, A, E, O, C, M, N, S, T, Y

Using the above letters, the player could make: CANOE and MAST. The Y is left over.

Game variations

♦ Not all the letters are shared out to start with. Some are kept face down in a pile. Once players have used their cards to make as many words as possible, they can take turns to pick up another card and, with the help of that card, put down the rest of their letters. Players can also change words that they have already put down. The game ends when the first player runs out of cards. If any player is unable to put down all of his cards, players could agree to find a space for his left-over letters by adding them to others' words.

Another option is that the players could swap cards with their neighbours once all of the letters have been shared out. They then take turns to pick a card without looking at it.

◆ Instead of simply putting down individual words under, or next to, each other, the letter cards could also be put together like a crossword. The players could either make up their own crossword or create a group crossword.

◆ The game can be made more difficult if the words have to be of a particular type (eg, nouns), or belong to a particular category or subject.

For the basic version of this game, the winner is the player who is first to put down all their letters, or who has the least number of letters left over. Alternatively, points could be given for the number, length or originality of the words made. Points could be deducted for unused letters. This can make the game more challenging and opens up chances for different players to win.

19 Letter travel

One player thinks of a place that he would like to travel to, but only names the first letter. The next player now has to guess the second letter, then the next player the third, and so on. Whoever thinks they can guess the complete place name, says so. If his guess is wrong, that player is out, or has a point deducted. For example,

The first player says: 'I am travelling to B...'
(*He is thinking Bristol.*)

The second player says: 'I am travelling to Br...'
(*He is thinking of Braintree, but is allowed to continue playing, because Bristol also has an R as its second letter.*)

The third player says: 'I am travelling to Bra...'
(*Like the second player, he is thinking of Braintree, but is out or is given a minus point, because the third letter of Bristol is not an A.*)

The fourth player says: 'I am travelling to Bri...'
(*It does not matter if he is thinking of Brighton, Bridgewater, etc: the 'I' in third place is definitely correct.*)

Game variations
◆ Instead of towns and cities, players could also guess countries.

◆ In order to make the game a little easier, the number of syllables of the word to be guessed could be given in advance and information about the county or country in which the town or city could be provided.

◆ Instead of towns and cities or countries, players could guess another category of long words. For example 'I am eating a piece of s…'.

20 Letter Rummy

For this game, you will need 104 cards with the following letters (two old card decks could be used):

A×8	H×4	O×6	V×3
B×3	I×7	P×3	W×3
C×3	J×3	Q×1	X×1
D×3	K×3	R×6	Y×2
E×8	L×3	S×6	Z×2
F×3	M×4	T×6	
G×3	N×4	U×6	

In addition add four to six jokers.

Playing this game is similar to playing number Rummy, but instead of putting down the same numbers or number sequences, the players have to put down singular nouns: any player who can make a complete word using a minimum of four cards, can put these cards down. To begin with, a small number of cards is shared out among the players, then they take it in turns to pick up a card from a pile lying face down, and to throw away a card in their hands that they think they do not need. Any player who puts down at least one word is allowed to put down cards to extend that word or add to the other players' words, as long as the newly created word is a meaningful one. The game is finished when one player is able to put down all their cards, or when the pile of cards has run out.

Game variations

◆ Players are only allowed to put down words of a specific type: for example, geographical terms, first names or verbs.

◆ Alternatively, before the game begins, a particular topic is agreed and all of the words have to belong to this group: for example, 'party time' or 'birthday'.

Points can be deducted for each card that players are still holding in their hands at the end of the game. Alternatively, points could be given for each letter which is put down, with additional points for each word created.

(21) Letter salad

Individual letters of chosen words are mixed up. Players then have to try to guess the original words:

giter: tiger
esetilvoin: television
trunsthomred: thunderstorm

Game variations

◆ Make the game easier by providing the initial letter of the word to be found.

◆ Make it more difficult by mixing up letters of two words with each other. For example: 'ham' and 'nite' are deciphered as 'hit' and 'name'.

The winner is the person who is able to put the two correct words together first. Players should play in teams, to ensure that those with less developed language skills also have a chance.

22 Letter riddles

The group leader starts by asking members of the group some riddles and players have to answer these verbally, or in writing. After a while, it is likely that the players will begin to think of suitable letter-riddles. Players then take it in turns to make up riddles for the rest of the group to solve. For example:

What did yesterday start with and Sunday finish with?
a 'Y'

What is the same for dawn and dusk?
the 'D'

Two architects want to build a house – what does each start with?
an 'E'

What is in the middle of Paris?
an 'R'

Finding new questions can be more fun than answering them. If the game is played as a competition, the originality of the question could always be discussed, as well as the answers that are given.

(23) The secret of the four letters

The group leader thinks of a long word that will be familiar to the group. From this a mysterious sounding sequence of four letters is selected (the letters have to stay in the same order as they were in the original word), written on a piece of paper and shown to the other players. They now try to find the original word as quickly as possible. For example:

> The word the group leader is thinking of is str**awbe**rry.

> The sequence selected and shown to the other players is: **awbe**

From this, the players have to try and guess the original word. If necessary, clues could be given. In this case, 'a fruit', 'red in colour', 'eaten with cream'.

Game variations
- ◆ Players try to build as many words as possible containing the given letter sequence.

- ◆ The group of letters from which players have to guess a word could contain more than four letters.

> The winner is the player who thinks of the original word first. Alternatively, points could be given for each word, and the player who guesses the most original words is the winner.

24 'M' in the middle

Within a given time, the players try to find as many words as possible that have an 'm' or more than one 'm' in the middle:

ca **m** el

ha **mm** er

ta **m** er

Game variations

◆ Various letters of the alphabet could be specified as a middle point.

◆ Make the game more difficult by choosing two letters, for example, 'nd':

fi **nd** er

blu **nd** ers

Mo **nd** ay

Points can be given for any unusual words, for the number of words found, or possibly for the number of letters that come in front of, and after, the middle two letters.

25 The 'you' game

Players have to find as many words as possible that start with 'you', such as: your, youth, yourself.

Game variation

◆ Players are allowed to include words that start with the letters 'you', but are pronounced differently, such as: young or youngster.

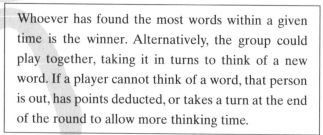

Whoever has found the most words within a given time is the winner. Alternatively, the group could play together, taking it in turns to think of a new word. If a player cannot think of a word, that person is out, has points deducted, or takes a turn at the end of the round to allow more thinking time.

26 The longest sentence

A sentence consisting of only a subject and a predicate is given. The sentence is expanded by adding a word anywhere in the sentence, in order to make a sentence that is as long as possible without introducing a subordinate clause.

The water is running.
The water is running fast.
The cold water is running fast.
The icy, cold water is running fast.

Game variations

◆ Players can add subordinate clauses.

◆ Players can also add two words at a time. For example:

The water is running.
The very cold water is running.
The very cold water is running extremely fast.
The very cold, icy water is running extremely fast downhill.

Whoever has made the longest sentence within a given time, or whoever has thought of the most original sentence is the winner.

(27) Peter does not like sweets

The title of this game can be used as part of a trial run, so that players can discover how the game works. The group leader begins by saying: 'Peter does not like sweets, but he does like a lollipop'. The players now take turns to ask questions about people, objects and activities that Peter likes, or does not like, in order to discover what it is that Peter does not like. The group leader answers each question with 'yes' or 'no'. For example:

Does Peter like crisps?
No, he does not like crisps.

Does he like fruit juice?
No, he does not like fruit juice.

Does he like soda?
No, he does not like soda either.

Does he like drinking?
Yes, he likes drinking.

Does he like eating bananas?
Yes, he likes eating bananas.

Does he like driving?
Yes, he likes driving.

The answer is that Peter does not like anything that contains any of the letters in the word 'sweets', ie, the letters 's', 'w', 'e' and 't'. He likes everything else (ie, all other letters). Players who have worked out what is going on do not have to say what they think is happening, but can carry on playing and have some fun. It can take a while until the last person has worked out the answer.

Game variations

◆ Any sentence can be used to start the game. The game becomes more difficult if the word that dictates the 'liking' and 'not liking', contains as many different letters as possible, and not much is left to be 'liked'. With such difficult words the game will still be fun, even when everybody knows how to play it. For example: 'The farmer does not like the harvest.' Players take turns to name something that the farmer does like. Players who are not fast enough or give the wrong answer have a point deducted. The farmer could like 'fun', 'fog', 'dogs', and so on.

◆ Instead of taking turns to think of a word, players could agree that everybody has to write down a certain number of words listing things that the farmer likes.

Correct or particularly original answers are rewarded with a point.

28 Big chunks

Players look for words that contain as many consecutive consonants as possible, such as:

school, too**thbr**ush, li**ghth**ouse …

Game variation

◆ The number of consonants is set at two, three, four, or perhaps even five.

Points are given for the number of words found within a given time, and perhaps also for their originality.

29 Double meanings

A number of verbs are given in the infinitive by the group leader. Players create a sentence using the verb. They then have to write a sentence using the verb as another part of speech, which gives the word another meaning (for example, the word 'clearing' in the first example has two meanings depending on whether it isused as a verb or a noun):

to clear	The fog is clearing.
	There was a clearing in the forest.
to like	I like dogs.
	It looks like rain.
to see	The cat saw the mouse.
	He cut the wood with a saw.

Game variations

◆ Players think of verbs which can be adapted to mean something else.

◆ The game can also be played in reverse. Words are given, their double meanings explained, and players have to think of the original infinitive verb form.

Points are given for the number of solutions found, or for the speed with which they are found. Players can also play this game together as a group, without winners or losers.

(30) The ten-word story

Players randomly call out ten nouns. If a newspaper is to hand, the nouns could be selected from it at random. Then a story has to be written, incorporating the chosen words in any order. No further nouns may be used, but players can use any other part of speech. For example:

Nouns:
cow, house, window, grass, street, Paris, army, reward, man, strike

The following story could be created:
During a strike in a street in Paris, the army found a man feeding his cow grass from his house window as a reward.

Game variation

♦ The words have to be used in the order in which they were called out or found in the paper. For example:

> The cow from the house without windows ate grass in a street in Paris, which was used by the army to store a reward for a man who refused to go on strike.

The winner could either be the player who finishes writing the story first, or a prize could be given to the player who writes the most original and/or the shortest story.

The minister's cat

The group leader starts by saying 'The minister's cat is an arrogant cat'. Then the other players have to find as many characteristics for the cat as possible, all beginning with 'a'. For example:

angry – average – alien – able – adopted – abysmal

Game variations

◆ Instead of an 'arrogant cat', the minister could have a 'brown suitcase' (or anything else). The players then have to find characteristics that might describe a suitcase: beautiful, black, brand, new, blue and so on.

◆ Instead of looking for adjectives beginning with a particular letter, players could work their way through the alphabet:

> *The minister's cat is a(n)*
> arrogant, average, able, … cat.
> bad, biting, blind, … cat.
>
> *Finishing with:*
> zany, zealous, zippy, … cat.

Points are given either for the number of characteristics found within a given time, or for their originality.

32) Three letters – one word

Players make words containing three letters that have been randomly selected by the game leader. The words should be as short as possible and contain the chosen letters in a fixed order. The three letters do not have to be consecutive in the words and other letters can be used. For example, the letters 'L', 'O' and 'T' are given.

Using these letters, players could make the following words:

g**lo**at – **lo**st– s**lot** – **lot**to

Game variations

◆ Make the game easier by allowing the player to use the chosen letters in any order they like.

◆ In addition to changing the letters used, the game can also be modified by setting a time limit for finding as many words as possible, and presenting the number of additional letters which may be used.

With the basic version of the game, the player who has used the smallest number of additional letters scores the highest. When playing the other variations, points could be given for the number of words found within a given time, with additional points given for those words that have been found by only one, or just a few, players.

33 Three times five

All players make three sentences containing at least five words that start with consecutive letters of the alphabet in the correct sequence. The first sentence does not necessarily have to begin with the letter A. Before they begin to play, the players can agree to leave out difficult letters, such as Q, X, or Z. For example:

Andrew bashes colourful, delicate eggs.

Great headlines infuriated jocular kidnappers last Monday night.

On pavements quiver restless singers.

Game variations

◆ Players are allowed to leave out letters between sentences.

◆ Players have to make three different sentences whose words all start with the same initial letters.

◆ Sentences have to consist of a given number of words.

Depending on the variation played, players are judged according to whether they have managed to stick to the appropriate rules. In addition, the originality of each sentence is assessed.

(34) **Rule of three**

Each player writes a complete story consisting of only three sentences. For example:

> The sun is shining. However, I am shivering. It is cold.

> *or*

> The dog was barking. I gave him some food. Now he is full.

Together, the group decides whether or not – and how well – the three-sentence stories have worked out.

Game variations

◆ The game can be played within a set time limit.

◆ Story topics could be given.

◆ Instead of three-sentence stories, players could also write four- or five-sentence stories.

(35) Dippy as a doughnut

One player selects a letter. The other players then have to choose an insult consisting of an adjective and a noun, both of which have to begin with the chosen letter. For example:

D: You **d**ippy **d**oughnut!

R: You **r**ude **r**ascal!

U: You **u**gly **u**rchin!

Game variations

◆ Instead of insults the players could give compliments:

A: You **a**ble **a**ngel!

D: You **d**azzling **d**iamond!

S: You **s**elfless **s**oul mate!

◆ Substitute the same letter for letter combinations. For example,

'C' for the adjective and 'L' for the noun:

You **c**hirpy **l**emon!

You **c**umbersome **l**ump!

You **c**ute **l**ove!

You **c**lever **l**ady!

The game is fun in its own right, and there is no need to decide on winners and losers. However, if the players want to play competitively, points could be given for the uniqueness or the originality of the silly sayings.

36 Filling in the gaps

The group leader prepares a text containing as many nouns as possible. A gap is left before each noun for the players to insert adjectives. Players have to complete the text using adjectives that make sense and are as original as possible. For example:

The given text goes like this:

One ... evening, a ... man went into the ... forest. Under a ... tree the ... walker found a(n) ... animal, which was holding a ... plant in its ... mouth.

The solution could be:

One rainy evening, a very old man went into the dark forest. Under a crippled tree, the venerable walker found a mythical animal which was holding a dark blue plant in its watering mouth.

Game variation

◆ Players split into groups and play against each other. The choice of adjectives is agreed within each group. Sentence construction of the text can be carried out by the players as part of the game. When this has been completed, the originality of each word or story is evaluated.

(37) One at the front – one at the back

Players create meaningful new words by adding a letter both to the beginning and end of a word. For example:

in	and	ate
hint	**hands**	**water**

Game variations

◆ A word is given. The players have to create as many different words as possible by adding different letters to the front and back of that word. For example:

as
b**as**s
b**as**e
l**as**t
l**as**s
c**as**h

◆ Instead of playing individually, groups of players could play each other.

Depending on what has been agreed before the game starts, the winner is the player who finds the most new words within a given time, or who is the fastest to find a specific number of words. Alternatively, points could be given for the cleverest words.

(38) One-syllabic

During this game, players are not allowed to answer questions using the words 'yes' and 'no'. Instead, they are only allowed to use one-syllable words to paraphrase their answers. For example:

Did you like the cake?
It was nice.
Are you going to bed early tonight?
I am not that good.
Are you going to watch television tonight?
I do not know what is on yet.

Game variations

◆ The game becomes easier if players are allowed to use one- and two-syllable words in their answers.

◆ The leader asks each player a question in turn, formulating them so that players are tempted to answer 'yes' or 'no'. If there are players of different abilities and ages in the group, the leader can even out these differences by varying the style of the questions asked. In this way, everybody can participate on an equal footing and have fun.

Points could be given for the number of words in the answer sentence – the more words the better – or for the originality of the answers. Alternatively, the group could wait together for someone to slip up and then laugh about it together.

(39) One word is always there

One player thinks of a simple word and writes it on a piece of paper which is kept face down on the table. Other players then take it in turns to ask that player questions about anything they like. That player has to use the chosen word in each answer. The game is over when one of the other players has guessed the word correctly. For example:

The word is 'have':

Player 1:	What is your word?
Answer:	I don't **have** to tell you.
Player 2:	What are you going to have for dinner tonight?
Answer:	Actually, I **have** absolutely no idea!
Player 3:	What is the time?
Answer:	I **have** my watch right here, let me check. It is ten o'clock.

Game variations

◆ The secret word has to be a noun, a verb, an adjective, or similar.

◆ The players play against each other. When they think they have guessed the word, they write it down. However, they are allowed to continue to ask questions until the agreed playing time is over and everybody has to hand in their written solutions.

◆ With older players, or with adults, the word to be guessed can be hidden in answers that are as long as possible to make the game more difficult.

The winner is the first person to guess the word, or anyone who manages to guess the word.

(40) A word becomes longer

A two- or three-letter word gradually gets longer by rearranging the existing letters and adding one new letter each time. For example:

as

sat

salt

lasts

slates

cat-less

tactless

Game variations

◆ Players choose the starting word together, then every player works on their own, trying to get a word that is as long as possible.

◆ The same method can also be used to create a number of words that make sense together (for example, a compound noun, an adjective, a noun and so on) building up into whole sentences. For example:

> at
> tap
> pant
> paint
> pay tin
> play tin

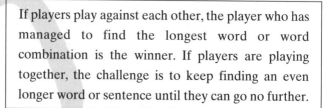

If players play against each other, the player who has managed to find the longest word or word combination is the winner. If players are playing together, the challenge is to keep finding an even longer word or sentence until they can go no further.

41 An additional 'T'

Players have to look for words that can be made into a new word by adding a specific letter anywhere in the word. For example:

The additional letter is 'T'.

tin – tin**t**
pain – pain**t**
he – **t**he
sub – s**t**ub

Game variations

◆ New words are created by adding two letters at a time. For example:

The letters are 'E' and 'R'.

the – there
we – were
sing – singer

◆ New words are created by deleting rather than adding a letter. For example:

The letter to be deleted is 'S'.

past – pat
stone – tone

◆ New words are built by doubling one letter – for example by doubling an E: we – wee.

The winner is the player who has found the most words within a given time, or who is the first to find a specific number of words. The game can be played without winners and losers if the group thinks of words together.

42 Little elevens

Every player writes a poem, consisting of eleven words distributed across five lines. For example:

Today	1st line:	one word
It is	2nd line:	two words
Very cold again.	3rd line:	three words
Hopefully tomorrow will be	4th line:	four words
Sunny.	5th line:	one word

The poems are read out – which one does the group like best?

Game variation

◆ A topic is given, for example, 'friendship':

> It
> Is nice
> Being with you.
> Hopefully it will last
> Forever.

or

> My
> Best friend
> Has left today.
> Perhaps tomorrow she will
> Return.

(43) False separations

Players try to create new words by segmenting common words into incorrect groups of syllables. For example:

talk-ing	tal-king
pin-stripe	pins-tripe
bar-stool	bars-tool
ro-mantic	rom-antic

Game variations

◆ Instead of new word combinations, players have to find words belonging to a particular category. For example, they might have to find as many strange animals as possible within a given time:

pen-ta-gram	pentag-ram
tra-bant	trab-ant

◆ Or strange body parts such as:

Po-peye	pop-eye
a-larm	al-arm

◆ It is also good fun trying to assign people to suitable occupations such as:

Bill Board, advertising manager
Lee Ming, Chinese translator
An Gel, hairdresser

Particularly creative players could put together an alphabetical name list, perhaps leaving out the difficult letters. For example, the list could begin with:

An Gel, hairdresser
Ben Efit, bank robber

and finish with:

Zig Zag, racing driver

The game is good fun without having to find a winner. However, if players want to compete, points could be given for the number of words found within a given time, or the speed with which a specific number of words has been found. Additional points could also be given for originality and imagination.

(44) Family research

Players have to think of different animal family relationships. For example:

What is the name of the child of a swan?   cygnet
What is the female partner of a pig called?   sow
What do you call the father of a foal?   stallion

Game variations

◆ Players think of relations in a human family. For example:

What do you call the sister of
a grandmother?   great aunt
What do you call the son of
an uncle?   cousin
What do you call the mother
of a grandfather?   great-grandmother

The game is easier if the group leader, or one of two groups, formulates the questions, and the other group answers. However, the entire group can also play together: one player begins by asking a question and choosing the person to answer the question. The person giving the answer asks the next question, and so on.

> Depending on the game variation played, points can be given for the number and/or speed of answers. The winner is whoever has the most points at the end of an agreed number of rounds.

45 Fire, water, air and earth

Players sit in a circle. One player begins by throwing a ball or similar object to another player, at the same time calling out 'water'. The player catching the ball has to quickly name an animal that lives in the water and call out another one of the elements, such as 'air', throwing the ball to another player. That player, in turn, answers with the name of a creature that flies in the air, calls out an element and throws the ball to a third person, and so on. The players are out, or have points deducted, if they name an animal that does not correspond to the given element, or name an animal where the element called out is 'fire'. Each animal can only be named once.

Player 1:	water
Player 2:	eel – air
Player 3:	robin – earth

Game variations

◆ Regardless of the element, the animal names have to begin with consecutive letters of the alphabet. For example:

earth – ant
air – bee
water – cod
earth – dog

◆ The game could also be played by groups playing against each other, with one group naming the element and the other group naming the animal.

The winner is the group which manages to keep on thinking of a new animal for the longest time.

Busy builders

Players sit in a circle. One player names the occupation of a person who makes a particular product. That player then calls out the name of another player who has to immediately name three items that are made by that person. The second player then has to name another occupation, continuing the game with the next player and so on. For example:

Player 1:	tailor
Player 2:	dresses, coats, suits – carpenter
Player 3:	table, bed, chair – baker

Game variations

◆ Players could also name items associated with different trades, such as tools. For example:

Player 1:	tailor
Player 2:	scissors, needle, thread.
	Carpenter.
Player 3:	saw, measuring tape, plane.
	Hairdresser

◆ If players are playing individually rather than in a group, the group leader calls out the occupations and everyone either writes down or gives their answers out loud.

Depending on the game variation played, points could be awarded for each suggestion, or deducted if a player is unable to think of answers quickly enough. Alternatively, the speed, quantity, or originality of the solutions could be judged.

Strangers in plural

The players have to find words whose plural forms double as words with new meanings. For example:

Torch (light) – torches, as in 'he sets fire to' …
Watch (timepiece) – watches, as in 'he watches television' …
House (home) – houses, as in 'to provide a home' …

Points could be given for the number of words found, or the speed at which they are found.

(48) Pronouns

Players find words that contain different personal pronouns such as 'he', 'she', 'we', and 'it'. 'You' and 'they' are best left out, since it is difficult to find suitable words. For example:

pit – us**he**r – w**he**n – **we**re

Game variations

◆ Players choose words of one specific part of speech, such as nouns.

◆ Players are only allowed to use words from a particular topic or category. The category, for example, could be food:

cheese – crus**he**d – **We**nsleydale - b**it**ter

Depending on the game variation played, points can be given for the number of words found within a given time, or the speed at which answers are given.

49 Hangman

The group leader thinks of an unusual word consisting of as many letters as possible and, on a piece of paper, draws a horizontal line for each letter. The initial letter is written above the first line and anywhere else it occurs within the word.

The other players now have to try to guess the word by finding the letters. For each wrongly guessed letter, the hangman grows a little, beginning with a mound of earth. For example:

The leader thinks of the word 'bareback'.

She writes down: b_ _ _ b _ _ _

The first player guesses D and the leader draws the mound for the gallows. The second player guesses A and the leader writes in the letters: b a _ _ b a _ _.

If the players guess the word before the hangman drawing is completed, the game starts again from the beginning, with a new word and a new hangman drawing.

Game variations

◆ Two players at a time play against each other. If the group is not too big, each player could play everybody else once. Words could come from a particular topic area, such as sport.

Points could be awarded for correct letters and deducted for incorrect letters. The winner is the person with the highest score. Points could also be awarded to those players who think of very imaginative words.

50 Writing poems (1)

The group leader shows a list of approximately five words to the players who then have to write a meaningful poem that has twice as many lines as there are words and contains all five of the words. For example:

The following words are given:

moss – grass – morning – ear – luck

The poem has to have ten lines and could read as follows:

Early in the **morning,**
Elisabeth gets up yawning,
And walks outside on the **grass**.
She pours some milk in a glass
And sits down on the soft **moss**.
She thinks about her boyfriend, Ross,
While looking at a duck.
She considers her **luck** and wishes
He was here
Whispering in her **ear**.

Game variations

◆ The words have to be used in a particular sequence.

◆ Instead of words, the players are given rhyming pairs at the outset, for example: morning – yawning; grass – glass; moss – Ross; duck – luck; here – ear.

◆ The poems have to be about a particular topic.

The finished poems are read out loud, without naming the authors. Then the players can judge which poem is the funniest, silliest or most original, or which was written with the minimum of additional words.

51 Writing poems (2)

Each player writes down any word they like on a piece of paper. Then the players get together in random groups of four. Together, each group has to write a four-line poem that contains the four words written down by the group members. For example:

The words are: you, weather, shame, amazingly

Using these words, players could write the following poem:

Today is **amazingly** grey
And **you** have gone away.
That is such a **shame**
And, what's worse, tomorrow the **weather** will be the same.

Game variations

◆ The words have to be associated with a particular subject, or perhaps a topic that is being discussed currently by the group, such as drugs. For example, the words could be: addiction, high, clean, dead. Using these words the following poem could be written:

Taking drugs leads to **addiction**.
Being permanently **high** helps you forget.
Being **clean** is what you aim for.
Being **dead** is what you might get.

◆ Writing poems may become easier if the players have to find eight-line poems instead of four-liners.

(52) Writing poems (3)

Players write any sentence they like on a piece of paper, ensuring that the sentence is no longer than one line. The last word of the sentence is written one line below the rest of the sentence. Then the paper is folded so that the next player can only read the last word. He writes a sentence whose ending rhymes with that word. Then he writes a one-liner. Again, only the last word is visible to the next player. The piece of paper is now passed around until it is completely covered in writing. For example:

Player 1: There are stars in the
          Sky.

Player 2: I really love apple pie.
          But what I like even more is chocolate
          Cake.

Player 3: I just can't stay awake.
          I am working too
          Hard.

Game variation

◆ A particular subject is given for the poem. For example, the poem might relate to a recent event, to the season of the year or to something equally pertinent to the group.

At the end, the completed poems are read out. No evaluation is necessary, as the poems were created through teamwork. Alternatively, players could discuss which poem is the most original, relates best to the given topic or makes most sense. But the attraction of the game really lies in the presentation of the poems.

53   Stuffed turkey

A long word is written down vertically, starting at the top. The same word is written again vertically, parallel to the first word but starting at the bottom. Players now fill in or 'stuff' the gaps between the letters as quickly as possible, making up words where the initial and final letters are determined by the letters of the long word. For example:

P	ai	D
O	tte	R
S	iest	A
T	al	C
C	a	T
A	tla	S
R	ode	O
D	i	P

Game variations

◆ The length of the words to be made up is specified, for example three letters:

T	i	E
A	i	L
B	o	B
L	e	A
E	a	T

◆ For very young players, or for people who are less able, the word could be written vertically only once and the players then have to find words that begin with the different letters. In this variation, the turkey remains unstuffed.

◆ A topic could be specified. If the vertical word determines the topic, this leads to particularly original contributions. For example:

The word is 'town' and all the words have to be names of towns:

T	aunto	N
O	akensha	W
W	aterlo	O
N	uthurs	T

Whoever finishes first wins. For younger players, everybody is allowed to finish. Points could then be given for particularly unusual words.

(54) Opposites

In this game opposites have to be found for given words. For example:

big – small	summer – winter
hungry – full	town – country
sister – brother	

Game variations

◆ The group leader provides a list of words. Individual players or groups of players try to find all the opposites within a given time.

◆ The group sits in a circle. One player begins by calling out 'big' (for example) and, at the same time, throwing a ball, or something similar, to another player. That player answers 'small'. He then says a new word, throwing the ball to a third person, who has to respond with the opposite of that word. If a player does not answer, or provides the wrong word, then he is out, or has a point deducted. If a player calls out a word whose opposite neither he nor the calling player knows, then the calling player is out, or has a point deducted.

Depending on the variation played, points could be awarded for speed or imagination, or, alternatively, the number of correct answers within a given time.

55 Opposites – slightly disarranged

Players think of opposites for part of a word, rather than the whole word. This will lead to nonsense words, which may have a deeper meaning. For example:

> greatly – smally
> sleepyhead – wakeyhead
> skyscraper – earthscraper

Game variation

◆ Players have to find compound words whose parts may be changed into their opposites. For example:

> great-uncle – horrible aunt
> daylight – night darkness
> hot dog – cold cat

Whoever manages to think of ten (or whichever number has been agreed before play starts) nonsense opposites first is the winner. Additional points could be given for imaginative words.

(56) Similarities

Two or more words are given. Players have to find out what these words have in common.

What do 'mountain' and 'valley' have in common?
They are both types of landscape.

What do 'Ruth' and 'Sarah' have in common?
They are both girls' names.

Game variations

◆ The more words given for a particular category, the easier it is to find out what they have in common. For example:

What do 'mountain', 'valley', 'hill', 'plain' and 'marsh' have in common?
They are all types of landscape.

◆ The game can also be played in writing. One group or the group leader prepares a list of words. The players write down their solutions.

The fastest player to answer correctly wins. Points can be deducted for incorrect answers.

Similarities – with a pinch of salt

The group leader names two objects or two people. Each player now has to write down three similarities between them on a piece of paper. For example:

What do a goldfish and a tomato have in common?
Both are living things.
Both are golden, when they are fully-grown.
Both need water to thrive.

What do a king and a monkey have in common?
Both have the letter K in their names.
Both are mammals.
Both aim high.

Game variation

◆ Instead of playing individually, groups of two or three players can play against each other.

After each round – that is, after each task, or after an agreed number of tasks – answers are compared. Points can be awarded for correct answers, and for original ones.

(58) Cryptic conversations

Players hold conversations using only words starting with a previously agreed letter. In spite of this, players still have to try and think of words that ensure the conversation makes sense. For example, if all the words have to start with G:

> George gone?
> Garage. Gambling game.
> Gasp! Goody-goody George gambling?
> Great gambling genius! Gone gaily.
> and so on …

Game variation

◆ instead of having a conversation, players ask questions, to which one-word answers have to be given. Instead of one letter, two letters are agreed on, and these must be used alternately as initial letters. For example, D and S:

> Does Sarah dance secretly?
> Daily!
> So, does she sing daily?
> and so on …

The attraction of this game lies simply in the playing of it. However, points could be given, depending on whether or not a sentence makes good sense, or whether the players manage to keep up the flow of meaningful conversation.

59 Sums

One player thinks of 'sums' that consist only of words. If the sum works out, the result is a new meaningful word. For example:

The sum is:
(air moving along quickly, minus beating everybody in a game) plus (the opposite of 'off') plus (a piece of metal, shaped so it fits in a lock) = an animal that looks like a small horse with long ears.

The answer is:
(wind – win) + on + key =
d + on + key =
donkey

Game variation
◆ Two or more groups play against each other. One group at a time prepares the sums for the other group(s) to solve.

The winner is the person who solves the word sum first. If several rounds are played, the players can agree a point system. The player who has the most points at the end is the winner.

(60) Hansel and Gretel

Players have to think of well-known pairs, such as:

Hansel & Gretel
Mickey & Minnie Mouse
Romeo & Juliet

It does not matter if the pairs are lovers, siblings or another type of pair; in fact, even Little Red Riding Hood and the wolf are a pair.

Game variations

◆ Instead of pairs, players could look for well-known groups, such as:

Snow White and the seven dwarfs
Tellytubbies
Goldilocks and the three bears

◆ The game can also be played as a partner game: the first player names the first person in a pair, the second, the match for that person.

Whoever has found the most pairs or groups within a given time is the winner.

61 Haiku

Players write haiku, a form of poetry from Japan. A haiku consists of three unrhymed lines of five, seven and five syllables. For example:

The purple Sonja	1st line 5 syllables
Is a fantastic girlfriend.	2nd line 7 syllables
Always, forever.	3rd line 5 syllables

Game variation

◆ A topic is chosen for the poems, such as forest:

In the green forest
I like to go for a walk.
The forest is great.

Marks could be given for imagination and speed of haiku composition.

(62) Draw & guess

For this game, you need a whiteboard, or a large piece of paper. Players might like to do their drawings on the floor, so that everybody can see them. The game leader shows each group member a word or expression that has to be drawn, and the other players have to guess what it is. The artist changes after every correct guess, until everybody has had a turn. For example:

The game leader shows the word 'envelope'.
The player draws:

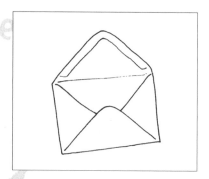

Game variation

◆ The game lends itself best to two groups playing each other. One member of a group at a time draws for their team, and the other group has to guess what is being drawn.

◆ With older groups, the game leader can make the items to be drawn more unusual.

If everybody plays together, points are awarded to the player who is first to guess the solution. The player with the most points is the winner. If groups play each other, the game could be timed and the players could be given a fixed amount of time to draw a word or expression. If the time is up before the other group is able to guess the item, the artist has to move on to the next word. The group which guesses the most items correctly within a given time wins.

(63) I am travelling to Honolulu

The group leader makes a statement about somewhere she plans to travel, for example, 'I am travelling to Honolulu'. Now all of the players write down how many years they are going to stay there, and what they are going to do while they are there. The number of years is determined by the number of syllables in the destination word (four for Ho-no-lu-lu). The verb used in each activity should use the vowel *sound* from the destination word, in sequence. For example: 'I am travelling to Honolulu. I am going to stay there for four years':

During the first year, I am going to lobby for justice.

In the second year, I am going to sort out my stamp collection.

In year three, I am going to lose my heart.

During the fourth year, I am going to sue the government.

or

I am travelling to India. I am going to stay there for three years.

During the first year, I am going to win the lottery.

In year two, I am going to bin all my old clothes.

During the third year, I am going to analyse my life.

Game variation

◆ The game becomes more difficult if the first verb used to describe the activities has to use the first combination of consonants and following vowel from the destination word, the second verb uses the second set of consonants and vowel, and so on. For example: 'I am travelling to Chesham. I am going to stay there for two years.'

> In the first year, I am going to **che**ck out the town. In the second year, I am going to **sha**re my house with friends.

Marks can be given for the uniqueness or originality of the solutions.

64 I spy with my little eye

One player thinks of an object that is visible to everyone in the room and gets other group members to guess what it is by gradually providing descriptive clues about the item. The winner is whoever says the name of the item the player is thinking of first. For example, one player (Player A) is thinking of a green plastic paper bin.

Player A says:	'I spy with my little eye something that is green.'
Player B guesses:	'Anna's green jumper.'
Player A answers:	'No, too soft. I spy with my little eye something that is green and hard.'
Player C guesses:	'The apple on the table over there.'
Player A answers:	'No, I spy with my little eye something that is green and hard and on the floor.'

Game variation

◆ Players must not say the name of the item aloud.
Instead, after an agreed time, they write their answers
down on a piece of paper. Points are awarded for
correct answers.

Instead of awarding points to the players who are
guessing, points could be awarded to the player who
has thought of the object. The winner is the person
who is able to distract his fellow players from the
correct answer for the longest time. To prevent
cheating, it is best for the player to write down the
item before the game starts.

(65) No – without

One player makes up a sentence containing 'no' and 'without'. The rest of the players now have to take it in turns to answer with a rhyme that also contains 'no' and 'without'. In addition, each player who has given an answer also has to make up a new sentence with 'no' and 'without', to which the next player has to respond with his own rhyme, and so on.

Player 1: No mother without a child.
Player 2: No tame without wild.
            No radio without sound.
Player 3: No circle without round.
            No purchase without money.

The rhymes can be silly, but should make sense.

Game variation

◆ Each player plays for himself. Within a given time, players have to find as many original rhymes as possible to follow on from the first rhyme.

> Instead of 'no' and 'without', the rhyme could contain 'no' and 'with'. For example:
>
> Player 1:   No ice cream with heat.
>
> Player 2:   No vegetarian with meat.
>
>   No child with a driving licence.
>
> Player 3:   No kitchen with a bed.
>
>   No worms with teeth.

Depending on the game variation, marks could be given for the number of rhymes found within a given time, or for their originality.

66 Small ads

A piece of paper is divided into three columns. The first player writes down an object, person, or animal in the first column, folds the paper to cover the writing and passes the paper on to the next player. The second player writes down a characteristic or a brief description of an object, person, or animal in the second column, folds over the paper and passes it on. The third player writes down what could be done with the object, person, or animal in the third column, and the advert is complete. The paper is then unfolded and the advert is read out loud. For example:

Player 1:   Small terrier …
Player 2:   only three legs …
Player 3:   to rent.

Game variations

◆ Groups of three players could play each other. The advert could be made longer by dividing the paper into more columns, giving information such as age, size, year of construction, quantity, and so on. The players could put together adverts with a specific content: wedding announcements, animals, items for sale or miscellaneous.

Marking for points makes little sense if there are only three players. The attraction of the game simply lies in creating the adverts. But if groups want to play against each other, marks could be given for the originality of the adverts, accuracy of expression, content, and so on.

(67) Body parts

Each player tries to find as many words as possible containing body parts, while never actually referring to real human body parts. For example:

Table **leg**
Nail **head**
Eye of a needle
Armchair

Game variation

◆ Players don't look for words containing body parts but another type of item, such as furniture:

Chairman
River **bed**
Table cloth

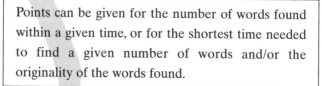

Points can be given for the number of words found within a given time, or for the shortest time needed to find a given number of words and/or the originality of the words found.

(68) Crossword game

The materials needed for this game are squared paper and coloured pens or crayons. In a school, the game could also be played on a blackboard with squares, using coloured chalk. Two players or two groups of players take turns to write meaningful words on the paper, one letter to a square. The beginning and end of each word should be marked with a thick line. The players or groups of players should use different coloured pens. The game is finished if no one is able to think of another word. For example:

```
R A I L W A Y
R           O
M           U
C           R
H O U S E S
A
I
R
```

Game variations

◆ A time limit could be agreed for finding a word.

◆ One player is only allowed to add in vertical letters, the other, horizontal letters.

◆ All of the words have to belong to a particular category or topic (eg, holidays, animals).

The winner could be the person who has added the most letters or players could count who has completed the most words. Alternatively, players could simply work together to try to fill the crossword grid as full as possible.

69 Cuckoo egg

One player thinks of four words, three of which should have an obvious relationship. The fourth is a 'cuckoo egg' (the odd one out) because it does not belong to the group, or go quite as well with the other three. The other players have to try to identify the cuckoo egg. This game needs some preparation, which can either be made by the game leader in advance, or become a component of the game itself. If the preparation is part of the game, each player, or group of players, thinks of (for example) ten groups of words, each containing one word that does not fit. Subsequently, the other players or groups have to identify the odd one out. For example:

House – building – tower – **fence**
Peach – apricot – **apple** – plum
Jumper – **glove** – blouse – shirt

Game variations

◆ All of the word groups have to belong to a particular category, agreed in advance.

◆ The players are allowed to use dictionaries, or similar reference sources, for particularly tricky cuckoo eggs.

The winner is the person who is first to find all of the cuckoo eggs.

(70) Shorthand

Each player has to write a story, containing as many numbers as possible which replace words, or parts of words. For example:

> 1 day, I saw a gr8 4tress. I 10sly went 4ward 2 see Manni2 and a man from 7oaks fight 4 their lives …

Game variation

◆ The minimum number of words in the story could be prescribed.

◆ As many different numbers as possible have to be used. In addition, other numeracy symbols could be used, such as: + to stand for 'and'; = to stand for 'is/are', and so on. For example:

> The 4finger of a h+ = gr8 4 scratching.

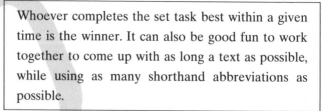

Whoever completes the set task best within a given time is the winner. It can also be good fun to work together to come up with as long a text as possible, while using as many shorthand abbreviations as possible.

71 Long words

Players work together to find words that are as long as possible. To do this, each player takes a turn at naming a new letter. For example:

> If the first player says K, the second N, the third O, and so on, the word could become 'knowledge', or even 'knowledgeable'. On the other hand, the word could also have become 'knockout' or 'knowable'.

The game is over when the next player is unable to think of a meaningful addition.

Game variation

◆ The game could be played as a competition. In this case, everyone is given the first and second, and perhaps even the third, letters. Each player, or group of players, now tries to develop these letters into a meaningful word that is as long as possible, within a given time. Whoever makes the longest word wins. Additional points could be given for very imaginative words.

(72) Magical word squares

Players make 'magic word squares' which consist of three or more rows and columns of letters. Corresponding rows and columns have to contain the same words. For example:

G I V E

I D E A

V E E R

E A R L

Game variations

◆ The number of words to be entered is given at the outset. The bigger the square, the more difficult the game becomes.

◆ One group puts together a magical square by means of a quiz. The words to be entered into the square are described, and the other group has to solve the riddles before entering the words. For the example above, the clues could be:

1 the opposite of take
2 your thoughts about something
3 to change direction
4 British nobleman

Depending on the game variation, whoever fills the square first, or solves the riddles fastest wins. Alternatively, when completing squares from scratch, marks could be given for words used in a meaningful way, or for originality.

(73) My name – my programme

Each group member writes their first name with the letters one under the other. Players now have to formulate words beginning with these letters and related to a particular topic. For example, Louis and Sarah could write down the following words related to the topic 'play':

L	udo	S	andpit
O	ut	A	ctivity
U	mpire	R	attle
I	dea	A	dventure
S	nakes and ladders	H	appy

Game variation

◆ Make the game more difficult by asking players to think of complete sentences rather than individual words. For John, these could be:

J	ump
O	ver
H	urdles
N	ow

(**74**) Pins and needles

Players think of as many popular sayings as they can, using as many pairs of words as possible. For example:

Pins and needles
Part and parcel
Spick and span
Rack and ruin
One and only

Game variations

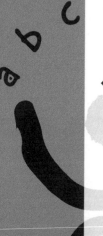

◆ The game leader reads out a list of ten to fifteen of the first words in paired sayings and all of the players write them down. Then each player adds the second word without any help from the others.

◆ Groups of younger players might find it easier if the group leader uses the sayings in a sentence. For example:

Toby said to Kate: 'I won this game fair and … square.'

◆ The types of pairs to be thought of could be specified.
For example, those that utilise:

> repetition of the same word: again and again
> repetition of meaning: stuff and nonsense
> opposites: thick and thin
> alliteration: rough and ready
> related words: body and soul
> similar sound: wear and tear

Whoever finds the most paired sayings within a given time wins. If the group is playing together, the object of the game could simply be to come up with as many paired sayings as possible.

(75) Monotonous sentences

The game leader specifies a letter by asking a specific question, such as, 'I hear that you have been to Brazil. What did you do there?' The answer consists of a sentence in which, with the exception of the first word, 'I', all of the words must begin with the initial letter of the country named by the game leader. For example:

> Game leader: I have heard you have been to Brazil. What did you do there?
> Player: I burned big, black, broken branches.

Game variation

◆ The number of words that a sentence contains is set before play begins: for example, in addition to the first word, 'I', each sentence must consist of five more words that begin with the same letter. The greater number of words to be found, the more difficult the game becomes.

◆ The game can be made even more difficult by agreeing that each sentence has to contain a word from a particular category. For example, a plant, an animal, a food item, and so on.

At the end of the game, points can be awarded for the originality of the sentences.

76 Writing news

Short news items are written in 'key word' style. To do this, a piece of paper is folded into six columns. The columns have to be completed, one at a time, by players who do not know what has been written by the preceding players in the previous columns (each player folds over what they have written so the other players cannot see it). The following information has to be written into the columns:

Column 1: what was the event like? (adjective, short description)
Column 2: who? (name of person, animal)
Column 3: when? (time reference)
Column 4: who? (object, name, type of person)
Column 5: where? (place reference)
Column 6: did what? (action word)

A completed piece of news could be:

cold-blooded Rosie Smith Easter Monday the shopkeeper at the central station smiled at

Game variations

◆ More information could be collected by increasing the number of columns: for example, additional people could be introduced and described briefly.

◆ The content of the news could be set: political news, provincial news, social gossip, sports news, economic news, and so on.

◆ Specific topic areas could be given: for example, all of the news items have to be related to World War II, Christmas or a thunderstorm in Devon.

If there is only one group, no marks are given. The attraction of the game lies simply in the production of the news itself. Alternatively, smaller groups could compete against each other. Points could be awarded for originality of news items, accuracy of expression, content or references to a particular topic.

77 New vowels – new consonants

Players have to make new words by exchanging all the vowels in a word for different ones. The selection of words to be changed has to be made carefully, since a complete exchange of vowels is only possible on rare occasions:

Latin could become **Luton**.
So**l**o could become **s**a**l**e.

Game variations

◆ Instead of vowels, players could exchange consonants, which tends to be easier. For example:

Butt**er** could become **r**un**es**.
Deer could become **f**ees.

◆ Players are allowed to change the order of the letters, which can make the game easier. For example:

So**l**o could also become **L**isa.
Butt**er** could also become **v**e**ll**um.

◆ Instead of just one word, players find as many words as possible based on the original word, within a given time.

Points can be awarded for the speed at which a new word has been made, the creativity of the solutions and the number of words found within a given time and their originality.

(78) New prefix – new word

Short, succinct words are changed by adding syllables at the beginning or end of the word. For example:

'Ant' could become:

tyr**ant**, gi**ant**, serv**ant**, and so on.

Game variations

◆ The number of syllables to be added is given. For example, the players are only allowed to use one-, two- or three-syllable additions. For example:

'Ant' could become:

assist**ant**, toler**ant**, complain**ant**, and so on.

Points could be awarded for the number of words found within a given time, the originality of the words, and so on. Alternatively, the winner could be the player who thinks of ten new words first.

79 Nine-times-nine stories

One player says a sentence and the other players write it down. This sentence begins a story which every player continues on their own. In total, the story must consist of nine sentences, with the fifth sentence being the climax of the action, and the last sentence, the ending. In addition, each sentence must consist of nine words. For example:

Game leader:

1   Henry has been given a bicycle for his birthday.

The story could then continue as follows:

2   He immediately took it to show his best friend.

3   However, unfortunately his best friend was not at home.

4   His mother did not know where he could be.

5   Unknown to everybody, his best friend had gone away.

6   Henry was sad and cycled home on his own.

7   He parked the bike outside his house and cried.

8   He never wanted to use the bike again, ever.

9   And that was the end of Henry's new bike.

Game variations

◆ The stories are written by everyone together. When every player has written their second sentence, they fold the paper to cover the writing, then pass the paper on to the next player; the next player writes the third sentence, folds it over, and passes the paper on, and so on.

◆ A story topic could be given, such as a thriller, a love story or a science fiction story.

Points could be awarded for the originality of the stories. If each player is writing for themselves, the winner could be the first person to finish correctly.

(80) **Not so monosyllabic**

The group leader provides a one-syllable word consisting of three letters. Each player has to try to find as many words as possible that contain that word. For example:

The word 'and' is given. The following words contain the word 'and':

h**and**, l**and**, s**and**, Engl**and**, hairb**and**.

Game variations

◆ No compound words are allowed, so this rules out the word 'hairband'.

◆ A one-syllable word consisting of four letters is given. For example, the word is 'back'. 'Back' is contained in: out**back** or **back**ache.

Whoever was fastest coming up with any word at all or who has found the most words within a given time wins. Points could also be awarded for originality.

81 Uncle Fred sings in the bathtub

Each player is given a piece of paper with six columns. Step by step, words are entered into each column to make a sentence: in column 1, the players write a family relation, rank, title, or similar; in column 2, a name; in column 3, an action; in column 4, a preposition; in column 5, a definite or indefinite article; and in column 6, a noun.

Each player writes one word in the first column, folds over the paper to cover the writing, passes it on to the next player, and then writes a word in the second column of the next piece of paper passed to him by his neighbour. He folds the paper, passes it on, and the activity continues in this way. Examples of sentences are:

Uncle Fred sings in the bathtub.
Mrs Dutfield climbs over the chair.

The last person unfolds the paper and reads out the sentence.

Game variations

◆ Different types of sentence structure, such as question or command, could be specified.

◆ The sentences could contain more than six parts: for example, the group leader could add place and time references.

◆ The sentences could relate to a given topic, such as a holiday by the sea, exams or a disco.

The attraction of this game lies in the originality of the sentences, which is a matter of pure chance. If several groups are playing amongst themselves, the whole group could get together at the end to decide which sentence is the funniest or most imaginative.

(82) Paradoxes

Each player writes as many paradoxical expressions as possible on a piece of paper. For example:

> The emperor lived like a king.
> A woman takes it like a man.
> The chess player threw in the cards.
> The cat led a dog's life.

Game variation
◆ The game is easier if the beginning of the sentence is given, and the players simply have to work together to complete the sentence in a paradoxical way.

In the basic version of the game, the winner is whoever manages to find the most paradoxical sayings within a given time. If the group plays together, they could vote for the most original sentences.

83 Looking for sayings

Players look for as many well-known sayings as possible, each containing a particular word which has been agreed before play begins. For example:

The sayings have to contain the word 'bee':
As busy as a **bee.**
Make a **bee**line for something.
You have a **bee** in your bonnet.

Game variation

◆ The players think of sayings that relate to a particular topic, for example, the topic could be food:

Know which side your bread is buttered;
Butter someone up;
Selling like hot cakes;
Teaching granny to suck eggs;
Salt of the earth.

Whoever finds the most sayings wins. In addition, points could be awarded for the most original sayings.

84 Guessing rhyming words

The group leader says, 'I am thinking of a word that rhymes with …', naming a rhyming word and writing the word she is thinking of on a piece of paper. The players then have to take it in turns to think of further words that rhyme with the group leader's word, until someone guesses the word she was thinking of. That player then becomes the leader for the next round. For example:

> *Group leader:*
> I am thinking of a word that rhymes with 'name'.
> *The word she is thinking of is 'frame'.*
> *The other players guess:*
> blame – dame – came – same – frame

Game variation
◆ Each player writes down their own rhyming words. After a given time, everyone checks to see who has found the target rhyming word.

> Points are awarded to the player who has found the target word. In addition, points could be given for the number of extra rhyming words the players have found, and the originality of rhyming words could also be marked.

85 R is recommended

Players sit in a circle and take it in turns to ask the person on their right a question. The answer must consist of one long sentence, in which all of the nouns begin with the same letter of the alphabet, recommended by the group leader. For example:

> *R is recommended:*
> How are you going to celebrate your birthday?
> I am going to go for a **r**un, have **r**atatouille with **R**uth, buy a **r**abbit, **r**un a **r**ace, listen to the **r**adio and look for a **r**ainbow.

Game variation

◆ The adjectives, and perhaps the verbs as well, have to begin with the recommended letter.

◆ Different initial letters can be chosen.

Points can be awarded for each word beginning with the recommended letter. Additional points are given for particularly funny answers.

86 Laying sentences

Words are cut out from old newspapers and stuck onto cards of equal size. The cards are shuffled and dealt out to the players. The players now have to use their cards to make up sentences that are meaningful and use up as many of their word cards as possible. For example:

One player gets the word cards:

however	luck	it	one
perhaps	decided	stayed	first
because	child	under	had

A possible sentence could be:
However, perhaps one child decided it had stayed under first.

Game variations

◆ Players are allowed to swap leftover word cards with other players.

◆ Each player adds word cards to other players' sentences, as long as the end product retains some sense.

> Depending on the game variation played, the winner could either be the player who has managed to make the longest sentence using their cards, or the player who manages to get rid of all their cards by swapping or adding cards to other players' sentences. Points could be awarded for the number of cards put down, and points deducted for any leftover cards.

(87) Sentence chains

One player starts the game by making up a simple sentence, for example, 'I have a hat'. The next player now has to make a sentence that contains the last word of the preceding sentence, although not necessarily using it as the first word of the new sentence. For example:

I have a **hat** – My **hat** is **great** – It is **great** to go on **holidays** – **Holidays** are my biggest **hobby** – My **hobby** is my **dog** – and so on …

Game variations

◆ The game can be made considerably more difficult by saying that the last word of the preceding sentence has to form the first word of the next sentence. For example:

I have a **hat**. **Hat** stands are **popular**. **Popular** music is what I listen to **most**. **Most** people like **chocolate**. **Chocolate** is what I would fight for with a **bat**. **Bat**man and Robin are my **heroes**. and so on…

◆ The game is particularly good fun if sentences end in words that have more than one meaning, such as 'bat'. The game continues until a player makes a mistake or does not know how to carry on.

◆ Players could look for sentences on their own and write them on a piece of paper, starting with a sentence and a description of the game variation to be played given by the group leader.

The winner is whoever has come up with the most grammatically correct sentences within a given time.

88 Playing charades

A compound word or short phrase is divided into its component words and acted out through mime and gesture. Half of the group acts out the words and the other half tries to guess them. After a while, groups swap roles. Words suitable for charades include: tablecloth, rainbow, eggcup, football, and so on.

> The winner is the group who can solve the most charades within a given time.

(89) Headlines

Headlines are cut out of old newspapers and magazines. Each player selects one of these without looking and writes a small news item to accompany the headline.

Game variation

◆ Individual players or groups that are not (yet) proficient writers are allowed to read out their stories.

90 Quick thinkers

The names of categories of nouns (eg, flowers, trees, mammals, rivers, etc.) are written on individual small cards. The cards are shuffled. A letter from the alphabet is chosen. The group leader picks up the first card from the pile and calls out the category. Now all of the players have to try to find an item from that category which starts with the given letter as quickly as possible. Then the next category is called out, and so on, until all of the cards have been used up. A new letter is chosen for the next round, and the cards are shuffled again. For example:

The letter is T:
flowers – tulip; first names – Tina; rivers – Thames; clothes – T-shirt.

Game variation
◆ Instead of calling out the answer, each player could write it down. After each round, players compare their answers.

Points can be awarded for every answer, and points deducted if a player cannot think of an answer for a particular category. The player with the most points is the winner.

(91) Quick pondering

Sixteen random letters are written onto a large square consisting of four × four small squares. The square needs to be clearly visible for everybody. If a letter dice is available, players could take turns to throw the dice to determine the letters. Players now have three minutes to make up as many three-letter words as possible. For example:

C	A	R	T
G	N	D	I
E	E	B	F
O	T	S	U

car – and – sun – sea

Game variations

◆ Players have to build words of at least four letters:

cart – gone – bang – carts – card – cards

◆ Players are only allowed to use letters that lie next to each other, underneath each other or diagonally across from each other:

fit – car – geo – net – bus

The winner is the player who has found the most words within three minutes. Additional points can be given for each word that is found by only one player.

92 Syllable chains

Everybody knows about word chains where the next word has to start with the last letter of the previous word. The game becomes more difficult if it is played with two-syllable words, and the next word always has to start with the last syllable of the previous word. For example:

ci - gar
    gar - den
        den - tal
            tal - ent
                ent - ail

Game variations

◆ The game becomes more challenging if the type of word is specified: for example, the players are only allowed to use nouns, or have to alternate nouns and verbs.

◆ Players can take turns to add a new word. Points are deducted from players who are unable to think of a new word. They then have to start a new chain.

If players are writing down their words, points can be awarded for the length of word chains produced within a previously agreed time. Groups of players could play against each other to ensure that less verbally talented players also stand a chance of winning.

93 Syllable puzzle

Two groups play against each other. The aim is to create words from a given number of syllables. Each player in one of the groups thinks of a four- to six-syllable word and writes each individual syllable on a separate piece of paper. These are shuffled well and given to the opposing team, which now has to reassemble the word from its pieces as quickly as possible.

Examples of multi-syllable words:
En – cy – clo –pe – di – a
In – ter – na –tio – nal
Do – cu – men – ta – ry
De – mo – cra – cy

Game variations

◆ The number of syllables could be fixed at four, five or six. All of the players have to work together to find a word whose syllables have been rearranged into a nonsense word by the game leader.

◆ The game can be made easier if the first syllable of each word has been highlighted in some way.

If two groups are competing, the group who is first to reassemble all of its words correctly wins. Alternatively, players could play an agreed number of rounds, and points could be given for each round.

94 Menu

Players sit in a circle. One player begins by asking, 'What's for dinner on Monday?' The next player quickly responds by naming a meal that begins with M, for example, meatballs. Then he asks the next player, 'What's for dinner on Friday?', and so on. The players are allowed to repeat the days of the week, but not meals or food items. The menu could include:

Mondays: macaroni, marrow, melon …
Tuesdays: tomato soup, tortillas, trout …

Game variations

◆ The first two letters have to correspond to the first two letters of the day:

Mondays: mocha torte, moussaka, mousse …
Wednesdays: Welsh hotpot, weak tea, weird pasta …

The players could also enquire about drinks for the different days of the week:

Thursdays: tea, tangerine juice, tepid water …

Players who cannot think of a suitable word have to pay a forfeit, or are out. Whoever keeps going longest, wins. The game can also be played by writing the words down. In this version, points could be awarded (for example) for the number of meals and drinks individual players are able to think of within a given time.

95 Mirror images

Players find palindromes: words that read the same, front to back, and back to front. For example:

> Gag – Otto – level – madam – deified – Anna

Game variation

◆ Instead of single words, two or more words could be combined to make sentences that read the same when read from front to back, or back to front. For example:

> A Toyota;
> Desserts I stressed;
> Del saw a sled;
> Madam, I'm Adam.

Points can be awarded for the number and length of words, and extra points could be given for the originality of word combinations or sentences.

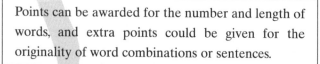

96 Sharp words

Players find words that all have a particular characteristic. The purpose of the game is to find as many original solutions as possible. For example:

The characteristic is 'sharp'.

Things that may be sharp are, for example:

needle

scissors

knife

tongue

remark

Game variation

◆ Two characteristics are given at the same time. It is particularly good fun to choose characteristics that actually contradict each other, such as:

Sharp and soft at the same time:

tongue

feather

piece of paper

Points can be awarded for the number and originality of the solutions. Alternatively, the players could just play together for fun, and simply try to find as many humorous things, with the specified characteristics, as possible.

(97) Guessing proverbs

While one player waits outside the room, the other players agree on a proverb. The player then returns, and has to guess the proverb by asking questions. Each answer has to include (as cryptically as possible) one of the words of the proverb, and the words must be given in sequence. When all the words have been named once, the next player is questioned and gives his responses, starting with the first word of the proverb again. The dialogue continues until the player asking the questions has guessed the answer. For example, the proverb is, 'Better late than never'.

Question: What did you do yesterday?

Player 1:   I got a **better** result in my spelling test than Sue.

Question: What is your favourite TV programme?

Player 2:   ER. I always watch it, even though it is on quite **late**.

Question: What is your favourite food?

Player 3:   The food I like more **than** anything else is chocolate.

Game variation

◆ A group of two to three players asks the questions. They are allowed to consult each other about the questions they want to ask and what the proverb might be. If the players are playing in a group, the proverb should be as long as possible.

Players could count the number of questions needed until a player or group has guessed the proverb. Points can be deducted for naming the wrong proverb.

(98) Town, country, river

Each player is given a piece of paper, which needs to be divided into three columns with the headings 'town', 'country' and 'river'. The group leader then names a letter, and every player has to write down a town, a country and a river beginning with that letter. For example:

The letter is 'T':

town	country	river
Taunton	Thailand	Thames

The letter is 'S':

| Salisbury | South Africa | Stour |

Game variation

◆ Additional columns could be added: for example, for flowers, animals, and so on.

The winner is determined by awarding points and players who find words that no one else has found get the most points. You might want to ask the players themselves about what sort of point system they would like to use.

(99) Synonyms

Players have to find as many synonyms (ie, words that are the same, or similar, in meaning) as possible for a given word. For example:

beautiful: pretty – attractive – gorgeous
rush: dash – hurry – hasten

Game variation

◆ The group leader provides a word list. Every player has to find a synonym for each word as quickly as possible.

◆ The group leader names a word. Players now have to take turns to find a synonym. Anyone who is unable to think of another synonym is out.

Depending on the game variation, whoever can think of the most synonyms within a given time, or whoever is quickest in finding a previously agreed number of synonyms, wins. Alternatively, the winner could be the player who has found the most appropriate synonyms.

(100) Teapot: double meanings

'Teapot' is a German game involving words that have double meanings. Two players agree a 'teapot' and talk about it truthfully, but also in as confusing a way as possible. The remaining players have to listen to the conversation and guess what the teapot is. Anybody who thinks that they have guessed the teapot can join in with the conversation, without actually saying the name of the teapot. For example:

The teapot is 'bulb' (flower bulb – light bulb):
Player 1 (flower bulb): My teapot is round and pointy.
Player 2 (light bulb): My teapot is round on one side and breakable.
Player 1: My teapot can also be broken, for example, with a knife.
Player 2: To cut my teapot, you would need a special cutting tool, but it is possible to cut it.

Game variations

◆ There are quite a few 'teapots' that have three or even more meanings, for example: the word 'game' could mean a sports game, a board game, to be 'up for' something, as well as animals or birds hunted for sport or food. Accordingly, three or more players can have a conversation talking about their teapots. The remaining players listen to the conversation. After an agreed time, each player writes down what they think the teapot is on a piece of paper. Points are given for correct answers.

◆ Instead of playing individually, players could play in groups against each other. Group members are allowed to consult with each other before agreeing on an answer.

Depending on the game variation played, points are awarded for each correct answer. After an agreed number of rounds, the points are added up to identify the winner or winning group. Instead of marking the performance of the players who are guessing the teapot, marks could be awarded to the players holding the dialogue. Whoever is able to confuse the other players for the longest time, wins.

(101) Teapot with a head

The group has to guess words that still make sense after the first letter has been taken away. Two players have a conversation and talk truthfully about their two words while, at the same time, trying to confuse the other players. One player represents the word 'with a head', the other 'without a head'. Any players who have guessed both words can gradually join in with the conversation, but they obviously must not say the actual words. For example:

The words are 'tear' and 'ear':

Player 1 (tear): My word is wet.

Player 2 (ear): My word can become wet when it rains.

Player 1: My word is soft and has no corners.

Player 2: My word is soft and hard and has no corners …

Game variations

◆ Players listen to the two who are conversing. After an agreed period of time, every player writes down the two words that they think are the solution. Points are awarded for correct answers.

◆ Instead of playing individually, the players play in groups against each other. Group members are allowed to discuss possible solutions before they write down their final answer.

Depending on the game variation, points are awarded for the speed with which players manage to guess the words. After an agreed number of rounds, the points are added up to identify the winner, or the winning group.

102 Text message

The group leader provides the group with six letters. Each player now has to put together a meaningful text message, using the given letters as the first letters of the words within the message, in any order they want. For example:

A A E G S T

Andrew **a**nd **E**dward **g**ot **t**here **s**afely.

Game variation

◆ The order of use for the letters is fixed:

A A H M M S

Anne **a**nd **H**amish **m**ay **m**arry **s**oon.

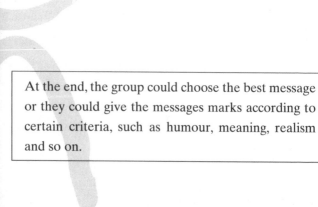

At the end, the group could choose the best message or they could give the messages marks according to certain criteria, such as humour, meaning, realism and so on.

(103) Words message

The group leader names a noun, a verb and an adjective with which players have to write a message, adding no more than seven additional words. For example:

Aunt – reserve – cold

Message:
Wish to reserve not too cold room for my aunt.

Game variations

◆ The words are chosen by the whole group.

◆ More than three words are given at the outset.

Points are awarded for the funniest message. Points could be deducted for each additional word used.

(**104**) Forbidden letters

The whole group invents a story which must avoid one particular letter. For example:

If the players are not allowed to use the letter E, the story could start like this:

On Monday, Anna saw a train. So Anna got on. Anna saw lots of things. Anna saw a …

Game variations

◆ The game is easier if a less popular letter, such as Q, is left out.

◆ The game could be played as a competition. Each player, or group of players, writes a story which is read out at the end. Simply writing such a story can be great fun, and often the laughter caused when reading out the stories is reward enough. However, in addition, points could be awarded for the longest and/or most original narrative.

◆ This can also be played as a 'question and answer' game. With the exception of the player asking the questions, players must avoid using a certain letter. If this is the letter A, for example, the group leader asks questions where the answers would normally involve an 'A word'. The question might be, 'What do you have a bath in?' The trick question is not answered by responding with 'water', or 'bathtub', but (for example) with 'in a liquid', or 'in a river'.

Players who use the forbidden letter are out, or take over from the group leader. A different letter should be made taboo every time the leader changes.

(**105**) Hidden animals

The group leader provides words in which the names of different animals are hidden. Players have to try to identify the hidden word as quickly as possible:

catch – g**rat**eful – sel**fish**ness

Game variations

◆ Two players at a time play against each other, taking turns to think of words by which the other player can identify the hidden animal.

◆ The players look for words that do not contain an animal, but some other type of word, such as the name of a tree. For example:

s**oak**ing – h**elm**et

Instead of one word, two words could be used to hide a word. For example, if the players have to find boys' names:

firs**t ed**ition – **tree s**tump

Depending on the variation, the winner is the person who has been most skilled at hiding or finding words. Alternatively, points could be given to reward both efforts.

Hidden numbers

Players have to find words in which the numbers one to ten have been hidden. For example:

onerous – **four**some – **ten**t.

Game variation

◆ Players find as many words as possible containing the same number.

Depending on the game variation played, points could be awarded for the number of words found within a given time, or the speed at which a given number of words was found.

(107) Business cards quiz

A name consisting of first name and surname is given. Players have to find out the occupation of the person, where they live, what they do, etc, by rearranging the letters of their name. For example:

Leo Broftal   What is this man's job?
                  footballer

Minah Grimb   Where does this lady live?
                  Birmingham

Betsi Warrser   What is this lady's favourite food?
                  strawberries

Game variation

◆ One group makes up the puzzle for the other group to guess. After an agreed number of rounds, the groups swap over.

Points are given for correct solutions and for the speed at which they are completed. If a player or group is unable to solve a puzzle, points could be deducted.

(**108**) Vowel sentences

Players have to make sentences consisting of five words which begin with the five vowels, A, E, I, O, U in that order. For example:

All **e**lks **i**nspect **o**ld **u**mbrellas.
Apes **e**at **i**ndigestible **o**range **u**rchins.

Game variations

◆ The five words of the sentence still start with the five vowels, but the players can choose their order. For example:

I **u**neasily **e**at **a**ardvarks' **o**ranges.
Unicorns **a**nswer **o**ld **i**llegible **e**nigmas.

◆ The sentences can have more than five words, as long as all of the words begin with a vowel.

If players are playing the five-word game variation, points can be given for the number and perhaps for the originality of the sentences found within a given time. If the rules allow more than five words, the player with the longest sentence will gain the most points, when one point is awarded per word. Points can be deducted for every word that begins with a consonant.

(109) Full house

A simple word is given. Players now have to find as many words as possible that can be combined with that word, in order to make a new word that still makes sense. For example:

The basic word is 'house':

house   – wife
         – boat
         – hold
         – work

Game variations

◆ The simple word forms the second part of the word. Players have to find as many words as possible that can be put in front of the basic word to make a new, meaningful word:

out   – house
full   –
boat   –

◆ Instead of compound words with the same words at the beginning or end, players could simply try to find words that include the same prefix or suffix. For example:

The prefix is 'contra':

contra – band
    – ry
    – diction

The suffix is 'less':

care   – less
guilt
home

Whoever has found the most words within a given time wins. However, the game can also be played without any winners or losers, if all of the players combine to come up with as many words as possible.

110 Heads and tails

Players try to find words that start and end with the same letter. For example:

Bo**b** – **r**udde**r** – **g**a**g** – **p**ul**p**

Game variations

◆ The initial and final letters are agreed in advance for each round.

Instead of individual words, players make up sentences that consist only of words whose initial and final letters are the same. For example:

Speechless Otto sponges yellowy stains.

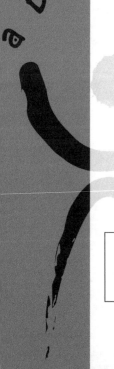

Points can be given for the number and originality of the words and sentences found within an agreed time.

111 What can you think of?

Seat the players in a circle. One player says a word and calls to another player, who thinks of an associated word and forms a sentence using both words as quickly as possible. That player then has to think of a new word, call to another player, and so on. For example:

Player 1:   winter

Player 2:   snow. Hopefully there will be snow this winter.

             sun

Player 3:   warm. The sun is warm.

             oven

Game variations

◆ The group leader starts the game by naming a heading or a topic, and the group creates a story around this.

When playing the basic version of this game, points can be deducted from players who are unable to think of an associated word, or cannot think of a sentence. The players could also play together, making up a story just for fun.

(112) What is romantic?

The players have to find new and, if possible, funny meanings for well-known words or phrases; alternatively, they could recognise the words or phrases from their descriptions. For example:

Goldfish: activity involving catching gold
Lipstick: small, thin protrusion from the mouth
Bookworm: small, snake-like creature, found in reading materials
Giant: a really huge insect that lives in colonies

Game variation

◆ The new word meaning could relate to an offbeat interpretation of the original word or phrase. For example:

Romantic – an ancient Italian city

Points can be awarded for originality, and perhaps for speed.

(113) Which proverb is that?

Each player writes down a proverb and then crosses out all of the vowels. The proverb (now consisting of consonants only) is written on a piece of paper and passed on to the player on the right, who now has to try to identify the proverb within a given time. For example:

Bttrltthnnvr
Better late than never.
Ltslpngdgsl
Let sleeping dogs lie.

Game variations

◆ Each player is given the same disguised proverb to solve by the group leader.

◆ Instead of using proverbs, players could guess the first lines of songs, or perhaps even German or French words. In the latter case, the English translation should also be provided to make things easier. For example:

splr – player
Spieler

prq – why
pourquoi

Depending on the game variation, whoever finishes first, or has guessed all puzzles correctly, is the winner.

(114) Who can think of the most?

The group leader writes down different letters on separate pieces of paper, leaving out the letters Q, X, Y, Z. There should be as many pieces of paper as there are players in the group. If the group is quite big, then it does not matter if some of the letters are used twice. Each player now randomly chooses a piece of paper and writes down as many words as they can think of that begin with the letter on the piece of paper that they have chosen. For example:

The letter on the paper is L:
lane – lamp – liquid – laurel – love – lies – litre – list

Game variations

◆ The players have to think of a particular type of word, for example, verbs. If the letter is M, the player could write:

    make – magnify – maintain – map – milk – must

◆ After the first round, each player has to write down as many words as possible beginning with the next letter of the alphabet. For example, if a player had R in the first round, he has to write words beginning with S in the second round, and so on.

◆ The player writes down a word of two letters, then three, four and so on until they can go no further. For example:

M: me, man, most, march, mostly, midwife, magnolia

The winner is whoever has found the most words within a given time. If several rounds are played, there could be round winners, as well as an overall winner.

115 If you were ruler of the world

One player asks, 'If you were ruler of the world, what would you do with me?' Another player answers, 'I would run with you'. The rule for this game is that the verb in the answer always has to start with the same letter as the noun in the question. For example:

A: If you were a **p**oet, what would you do with me?

B: I would **p**lay with you.

A: If you were a **f**ootball star, what would you do with me?

B: I would **f**oul you.

Game variation

- An adjective is added to the noun: accordingly, the answer has to contain an adverb beginning with the same letter. For example:

    A: If you were the **a**lmighty ruler, what would you do with me?

    B: I would **a**lways run with you.

> This is really a game without a winner, which can be played as a turn-taking game within the group. Whoever gives the answer, asks the next question. However, if a point system is used, then anyone who cannot think of an answer has a point deducted, or drops out of the game. In this case, the winner is the player who has the most points at the end of the game.

(116) Who can find the fibs?

One player from the group tells a story that has been so cleverly interwoven with fibs that they sound quite plausible. The other players have to listen carefully. Anyone who spots a fib is given a point. Points are deducted for incorrectly identified fibs. For example:

Player A: It was a really hot summer. It hadn't rained in weeks. On that day, my friend was coming to visit me and I was going to pick him up from the station. I had dressed smartly, so I was really annoyed when, just before I got to the station, I cycled through a puddle and splashed my new, white jeans …

Other players: Stop, lie! It hadn't rained for weeks, so there could not have been a puddle…

Game variation

◆ Players note down any fibs they have found on a piece of paper. Points are given for correctly identified fibs and deducted for those incorrectly identified.

Whoever has the most points after an agreed number of rounds wins. Alternatively, the narrators could be rewarded. In this case, the winner is whoever has managed to tell the most fibs undetected.

Who has the word?

Each player is given a word by the group leader. The words and their matching player names are written down in a place where everyone can see them, for example, on a flipchart or a blackboard. Then the leader begins to tell a story containing the previously distributed words. When one of the words is used, the player who has that word continues the story. For example:

The players are allocated words:
Player 1: far
Player 2: animal
Player 3: I
Player 4: went

Group leader: Last year, we had a fantastic holiday. **I** … [third player continues] drove south, as **far** … [first player] south as possible. We went on safari in Africa looking for elephants. The first **animal** … [second player] we saw was an old grey bull. He **went** … [fourth player]

Such a story can be never-ending.

Game variations

◆ Only nouns are given out.

◆ A topic is given for the story.

Points are deducted from the players who have not paid attention, or who are unable to continue the story. However, it is good fun just to let everyone tell stories without competing.

(**118**) Who is hiding in Parliament?

Players have to make as many new words as possible from the letters of a longer word. For example:

> The following words hide in the longer word 'parliament':
>
> lime – pat – men – rent – trim – map – tap – liar – male

Game variations

◆ Players make up only one type of word: for example, just nouns or adjectives.

◆ The words have to begin with a particular letter. Examples for 'parliament' could be:

> rat – ram – rate – rent – rip

◆ All the words must contain a letter chosen from the main word, for example an 'a', in any position.

◆ The game becomes easier and therefore more suitable for early learners when players do not have to work completely on their own, but if instead the group leader asks leading questions. For example, to help players think of a word that is 'hidden' in parliament, the group leader might say 'What looks like a mouse, but bigger?' 'A rat.'

Whoever has found the most new words within a given time is the winner. Words that have been found by other players either carry fewer points, or none at all.

(119) Who knows the paper?

Players have to find nouns that end in 'er'. They sit in a circle and throw a ball or knotted scarf to each other. Whoever catches the ball has to immediately come up with a word. For example:

paper – ladder – rider – singer – player – carer

Game variations

◆ The words have to start with consecutive letters of the alphabet. More difficult letters such as X, Y, Z, and perhaps Q, can be omitted. After a word beginning with the last available letter of the alphabet, the players should start again with A or work backwards to A. The players are not allowed to repeat words that have been used in previous rounds. For example:

   If the first word is 'mother':
   neither – older – paler – quainter – rather

◆ Instead of words ending in 'er', the players could look for words with different endings, such as, 'ing', 'ment', 'al', 'ation', and so on.

Players continue playing until someone breaks the chain because they cannot think of another word. If the game is played with pen and paper, marks are given for the number of words a player has found within a given time.

120 Who does what?

The group leader names some action verbs, and players have to find as many objects as possible which can be associated with those actions. For example:

shine: moon, lamp, candle, star, bald head ...
ride: train, bicycle, car, soapbox, wheelchair ...
fly: airplane, bird, kite, ladybird ...

Game variations

◆ The action verbs are provided as a list, and each player finds the related words on his own.

◆ Two groups play against each other, giving each other a fixed number of action verbs. To make the task more difficult, each group has to try to find actions that are as unusual as possible.

Points can either be awarded for the originality of the associated words or for the number of words found within a given time. Alternatively, points could be awarded to those players who continue to think of related words associated with the verb.

(121) How does it go on?

Players sit in a circle and one player starts a sentence. The group leader interrupts that player in the middle of a word. The next player has to complete the word and sentence so they make sense, but, if possible, in a different way to that planned by the first player. Then he begins another sentence, which is again interrupted by the group leader, mid-word. For example:

Player A: The sparrow sat on the win …

Player B: …ning horse. Yesterday it was rain …

Player C: … deer that I saw in the woods. At the station there were three people wai …

Game variation

◆ Players don't just make up random sentences but also try to tell a continuous story, which should be as original as possible. For example:

Player A:	The sparrow sat on the win …
Player B:	… ning horse. The horse's owner was wai …
Player C:	… ling because his horse had lost the race. A lady saw him and gave him a ti …

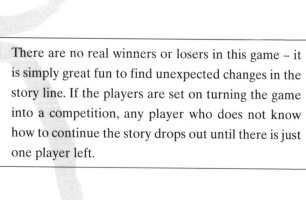

There are no real winners or losers in this game – it is simply great fun to find unexpected changes in the story line. If the players are set on turning the game into a competition, any player who does not know how to continue the story drops out until there is just one player left.

(122) What is your name?

The group sits in a circle and agrees upon one letter to start the first word of all players' answers. One player asks any other player, 'What is your name?' The second player answers, and then asks a third player, 'Where do you come from?' Once this player answers, he asks the fourth player, 'What do you sell?' Players can make up their own questions, but the questions should always ask for information about the other person. For example:

The letter is D:

Player 1:	What is your name?
Answer:	Doris.
Player 2:	Where do you come from?
Answer:	Denmark.
Player 3:	What do you sell?
Answer:	Doughnuts.
Player 4:	What do you earn?
Answer:	Dollars.

Game variation

◆ The game is easier if the questions and the order in which they appear are agreed upon prior to the game starting.

◆ The number of questions can be limited. Once the agreed number of questions has been asked, a new round is begun, using a new letter. A game leader asks the questions, and the players note down their answers. The answers are compared at the end of each round.

If the group is playing together, the winner is whoever is the last person to think of a question or an answer. If each player is playing for himself, points could be awarded for the number or originality of the answers.

(123) Hardening words

Players have to find words with a 'soft' (ie, voiced) G, D or B, which continue to make sense, even when the 'soft' letters are replaced by a 'hard' K, T or P. For example:

angle – ankle
bang – bank
bend – bent
bass – pass
dip – tip

It is quite difficult to find this type of word, so it is best for groups to play against each other. Dictionaries should also be allowed.

The winner is the player or group who finds the most words within a given time.

124 Guessing words

One player thinks of a word that has to be guessed by the other players. The player briefly describes the word, remaining as concise as possible, while still trying to confuse the other players. Then the others are allowed to ask questions, to which the player is only allowed to respond with 'yes' and 'no'. Whoever is the first to give the word is the winner. For example:

The word is 'pin'.

The player describes it as follows:
My word has a head, but it can't think.
It has no hands, but can be dangerous.
What is it?

Then the other players begin to ask questions:
Is it dangerous because it is poisonous? – No.
Is it big? – No.
Is it sharp? – Yes.

Game variations
◆ In addition to the description, the player could also provide the number of consonants and vowels contained in his word. For younger players, the initial and final letters could also be provided, especially if the word is a long one.

◆ Each player plays alone. Players are allowed to take turns to ask a question, then everyone writes down their suggested solution on a piece of paper. Points are given for the correct answer.

◆ Groups play against each other. Players agree on the number of questions each group is allowed to ask before they have to come up with a possible solution.

Depending on the game variation, marks can be given for speed of guessing, or for finding the correct answer within a given time.

(125) Where is Al?

Players have to think of as many words as possible containing the letter combination 'al'. For example:

Alan – **al**ligator – **al**arm – numer**al** – b**al**ance

Game variations

◆ Instead of 'al', players look for 'ben', which can be found in the following words:

benefit – un**ben**d – **ben**t

◆ Instead of looking for 'al' or 'ben' in single words, players could look for them in whole sentences. For example:

Alan **al**ienated m**al**functioning **al**iens.
Benjamin **ben**t **ben**eath **ben**ches.

◆ It is also easy to put together words with 're', for example:

reign – **re**gain – **re**ptile – t**re**nd – gen**re**

◆ Players could obviously look for words containing any letter combinations.

Whoever finds the most words overall, or the most words within a given time, wins.

126   Word treasure chest

In a box which serves as a word treasure chest, players collect words that have caught their attention, perhaps because they are particularly funny or strange. Such a word treasure chest can provide many ideas for play, for example:

> Each group member draws three words from the box and has three minutes to use the words in a sentence.

Game variation

◆ Instead of words, players could collect names of well-known personalities, cities, countries, musical instruments and similar items in their word treasure chest. Then one name is pulled out of the chest. Each player has to write a short text relating to that name. Who can think of the most to write?

127 Word snakes

Using two nouns at a time, players have to make up compound words in which the second part of the first compound word has to be the first part of the next. Players are only allowed to use each compound word once. For example:

goldfish
fishbone
bonehead
headroom

and so on …

Game variations

◆ Each player plays for himself. Starting from a particular compound word, everybody tries to build word snakes that are as long as possible, within a given time.

◆ The aim of the game could also be for the players to eventually end up with the original word, while adding as many words as possible in between. Again, a time limit could be set for this game.

◆ Players take turns to make up words. Anybody who cannot think of another word has a point deducted, or is out.

Points could be awarded for the number of words found within a given time, or for the originality of the words. If the players are playing for themselves, the winner is the player who has the highest score, or who is able to think of the last, previously unused, word.

(128) Word and number

The first player says a word and a number. For example, 'house' and 'three' means that the next player quickly has to call out a new word that starts with the third letter of the first word. Then he calls out a new word-number combination for the next player. For example:

Player 1 says:	'ho**u**se' and '3'.
Player 2 answers:	'**u**mbrella', and provides a new combination: 'ga**r**den' and '4'.
Player 3 answers:	'**d**etective', and gives a new combination: 'gia**n**t' and '4'.

Game variations

◆ The game is more difficult if players think of words that are as long as possible and use relatively high numbers.

◆ The group leader could be asked to provide the word-number combination, and the players could write down their answers on a piece of paper.

◆ The game could be played in groups so that players who have less secure literacy skills have more of a chance.

> Points could be awarded for correct answers and for the originality of the answers. Alternatively, players could simply continue playing until they cannot think of another word and number.

(129) Zoo in reverse

Players collect word combinations that contain an animal name. For example:

bookworm – scaredy cat – silly cow – scarecrow

Game variation
◆ Players look for word combinations that contain names from another category, for example plants (eg, family tree), or relatives (brothers-in-arms).

If players are playing alone, the winner is whoever finds the most word combinations containing a particular type of name within a given time. If the group is playing together, the aim is to try to find as many word combinations (including unusual ones) as possible, all related to one particular topic area.

130 Non-identical twins

Players have to find words that sound the same, but have different meanings, and then put them all into one sentence. The word must be used once as a noun, and once as a verb or an adjective in the sentence. For example:

The **cook** has to **cook** breakfast.
Mary **shed** a tear in the **shed**.
Did you see the **fly fly** around the room?
A **light** bulb is very **light**.

Whoever has found the most sentences in the shortest time, or whoever was fastest to find a specific number of sentences, wins. Additional points could be given for particularly original sentences.

ITV Be   10758 V

ITV 4   10.758   V 22. 0 5/

ITV 2 10.7

ITV 2 + 1   10891 H 22.05p

Fiver 10.964 H 22.00 5/6

ITV HD —
    11.053   H   3/4.

UTV HD — 11053 H 22 5/6

ITV Encore   10891 H

ITV Bet 1   10891 H

11052